WILSON

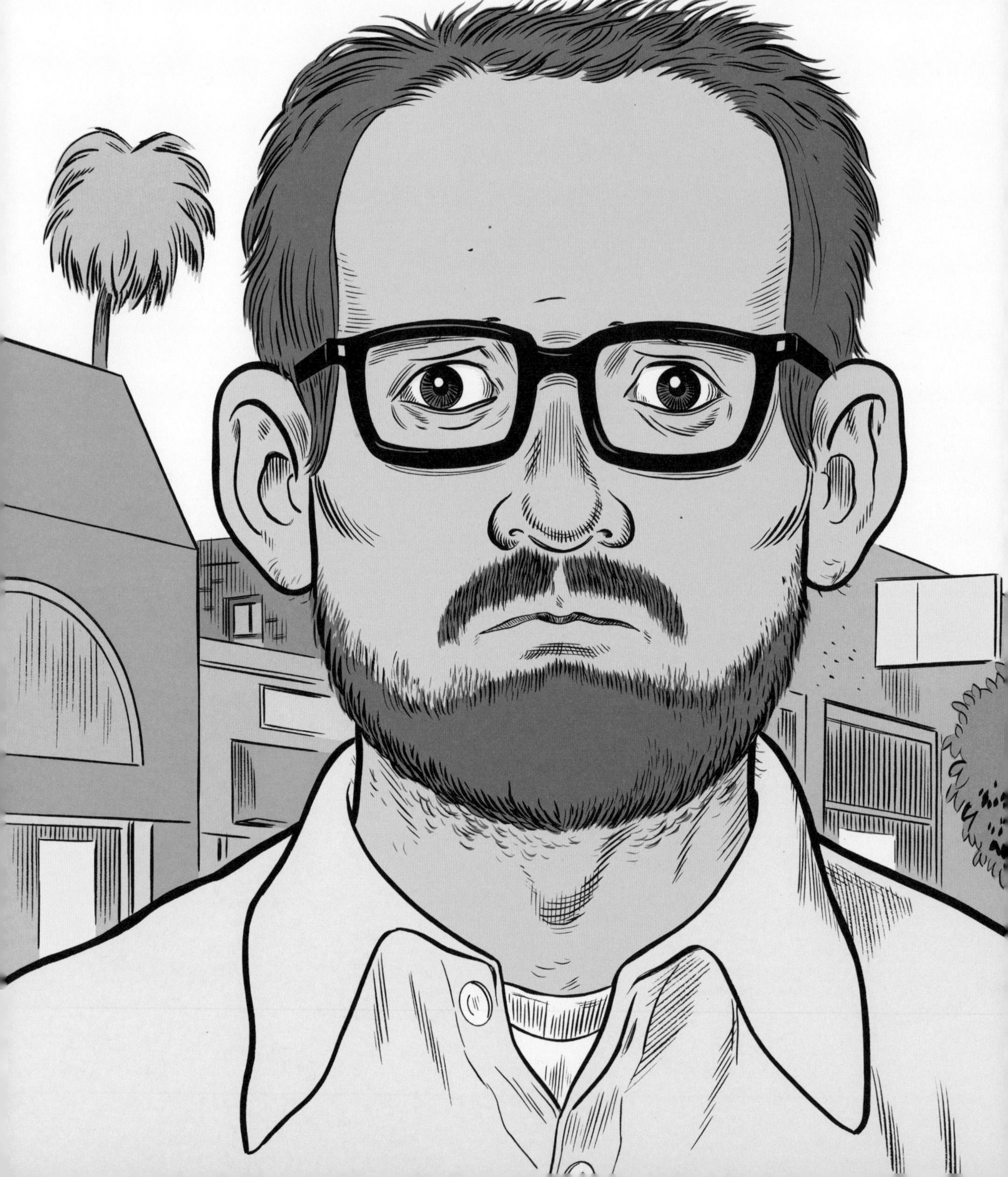

WILSON

BY DANIEL CLOWES

DRAWN AND QUARTERLY

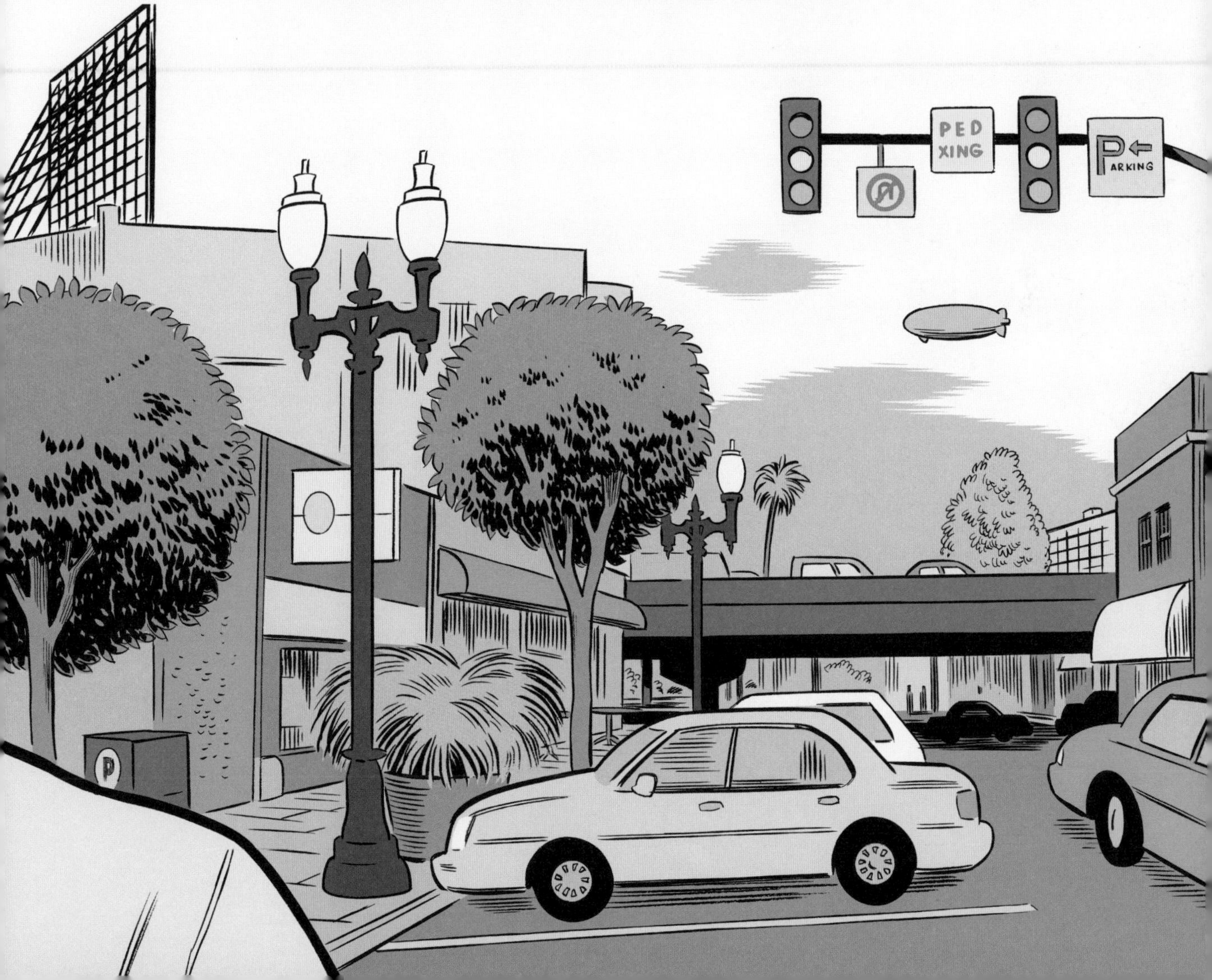
PED
XING
PARKING

TO GEORGE

AND, AS ALWAYS, TO ERIKA.

ENTIRE CONTENTS © 2010, 2015 BY DANIEL
CLOWES. ALL RIGHTS RESERVED. NO PART OF
THIS BOOK (EXCEPT SMALL PORTIONS FOR
REVIEW PURPOSES) MAY BE REPRODUCED
IN ANY FORM WITHOUT WRITTEN CONSENT
FROM THE AUTHOR OR PUBLISHER.

DRAWN & QUARTERLY
WWW. DRAWNANDQUARTERLY.COM

FIRST EDITION: APRIL 2010
FIRST PAPERBACK EDITION: APRIL 2016
PRINTED IN CHINA
10 9 8 7 6 5 4 3 2 1

LIBRARY AND ARCHIVES CANADA CATALOGUING
IN PUBLICATION
CLOWES, DANIEL, AUTHOR, ILLUSTRATOR
WILSON / DANIEL CLOWES.
ISBN: 978-1-77046-244-1 (PAPERBACK)
I. TITLE
PN 6727. C56W55 2016 741. 5'973
C2015-905504-0

PUBLISHED IN THE USA BY DRAWN &
QUARTERLY, A CLIENT PUBLISHER OF
FARRAR, STRAUS AND GIROUX
ORDERS: 888-330-8477

PUBLISHED IN CANADA BY DRAWN &
QUARTERLY, A CLIENT PUBLISHER OF
RAINCOAST BOOKS
ORDERS: 800-663-5714

WILSON

FELLOWSHIP

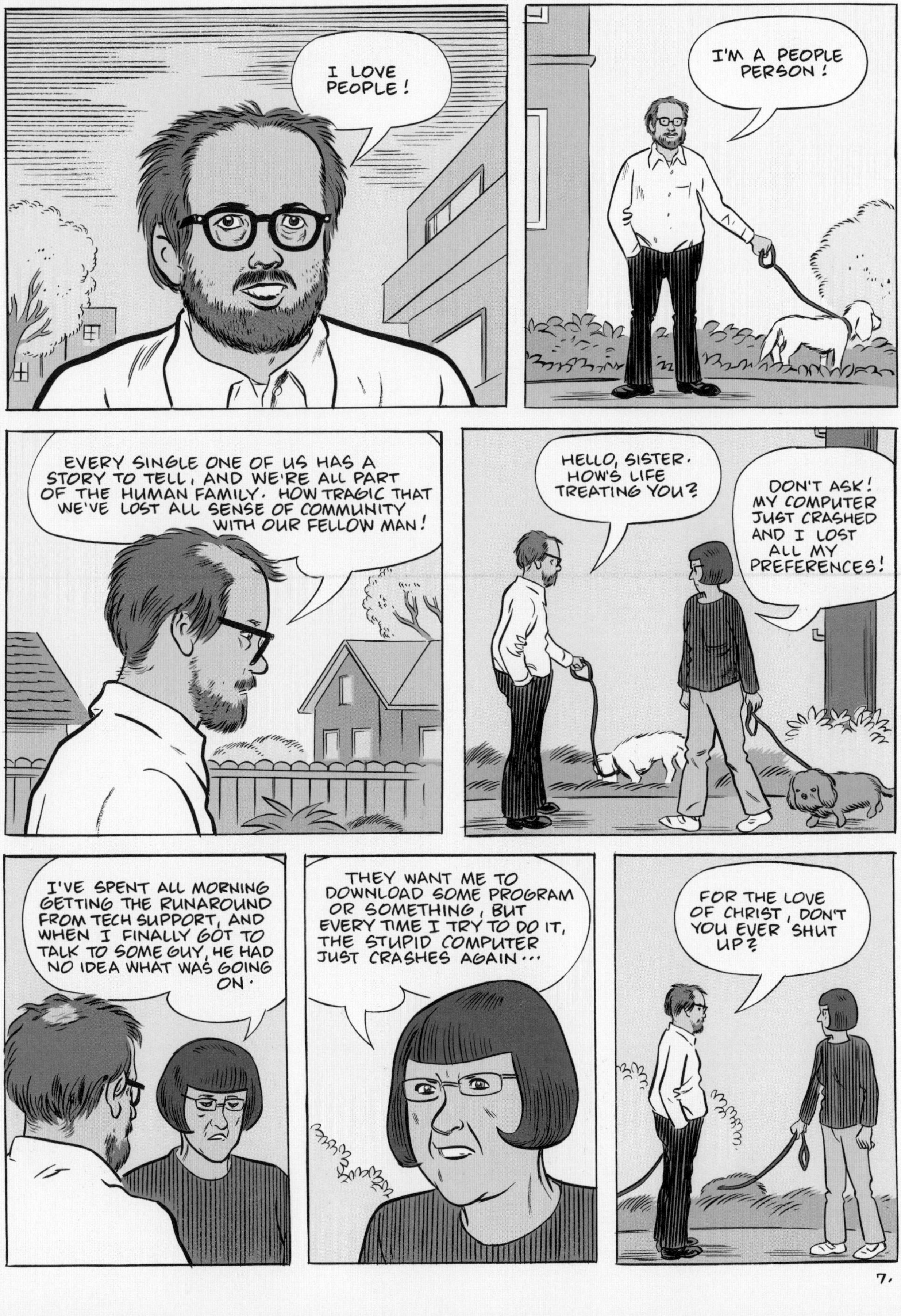
I LOVE PEOPLE!
I'M A PEOPLE PERSON!
EVERY SINGLE ONE OF US HAS A STORY TO TELL, AND WE'RE ALL PART OF THE HUMAN FAMILY. HOW TRAGIC THAT WE'VE LOST ALL SENSE OF COMMUNITY WITH OUR FELLOW MAN!
HELLO, SISTER. HOW'S LIFE TREATING YOU?
DON'T ASK! MY COMPUTER JUST CRASHED AND I LOST ALL MY PREFERENCES!
I'VE SPENT ALL MORNING GETTING THE RUNAROUND FROM TECH SUPPORT, AND WHEN I FINALLY GOT TO TALK TO SOME GUY, HE HAD NO IDEA WHAT WAS GOING ON.
THEY WANT ME TO DOWNLOAD SOME PROGRAM OR SOMETHING, BUT EVERY TIME I TRY TO DO IT, THE STUPID COMPUTER JUST CRASHES AGAIN...
FOR THE LOVE OF CHRIST, DON'T YOU EVER SHUT UP?

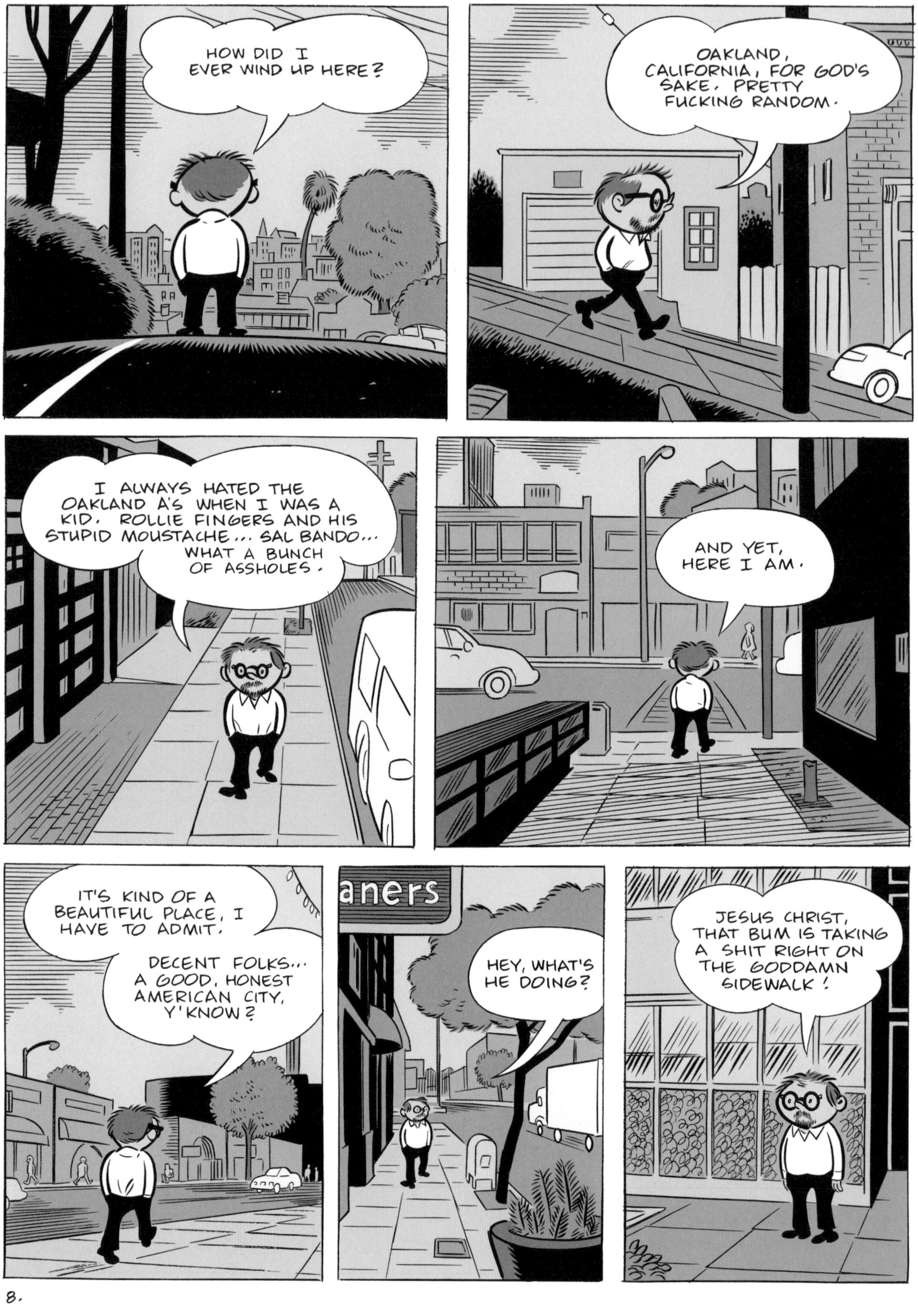
HOW DID I EVER WIND UP HERE?
OAKLAND, CALIFORNIA, FOR GOD'S SAKE. PRETTY FUCKING RANDOM.
I ALWAYS HATED THE OAKLAND A'S WHEN I WAS A KID. ROLLIE FINGERS AND HIS STUPID MOUSTACHE... SAL BANDO... WHAT A BUNCH OF ASSHOLES.
AND YET, HERE I AM.
IT'S KIND OF A BEAUTIFUL PLACE, I HAVE TO ADMIT.
DECENT FOLKS... A GOOD, HONEST AMERICAN CITY, Y'KNOW?
aners
HEY, WHAT'S HE DOING?
JESUS CHRIST, THAT BUM IS TAKING A SHIT RIGHT ON THE GODDAMN SIDEWALK!

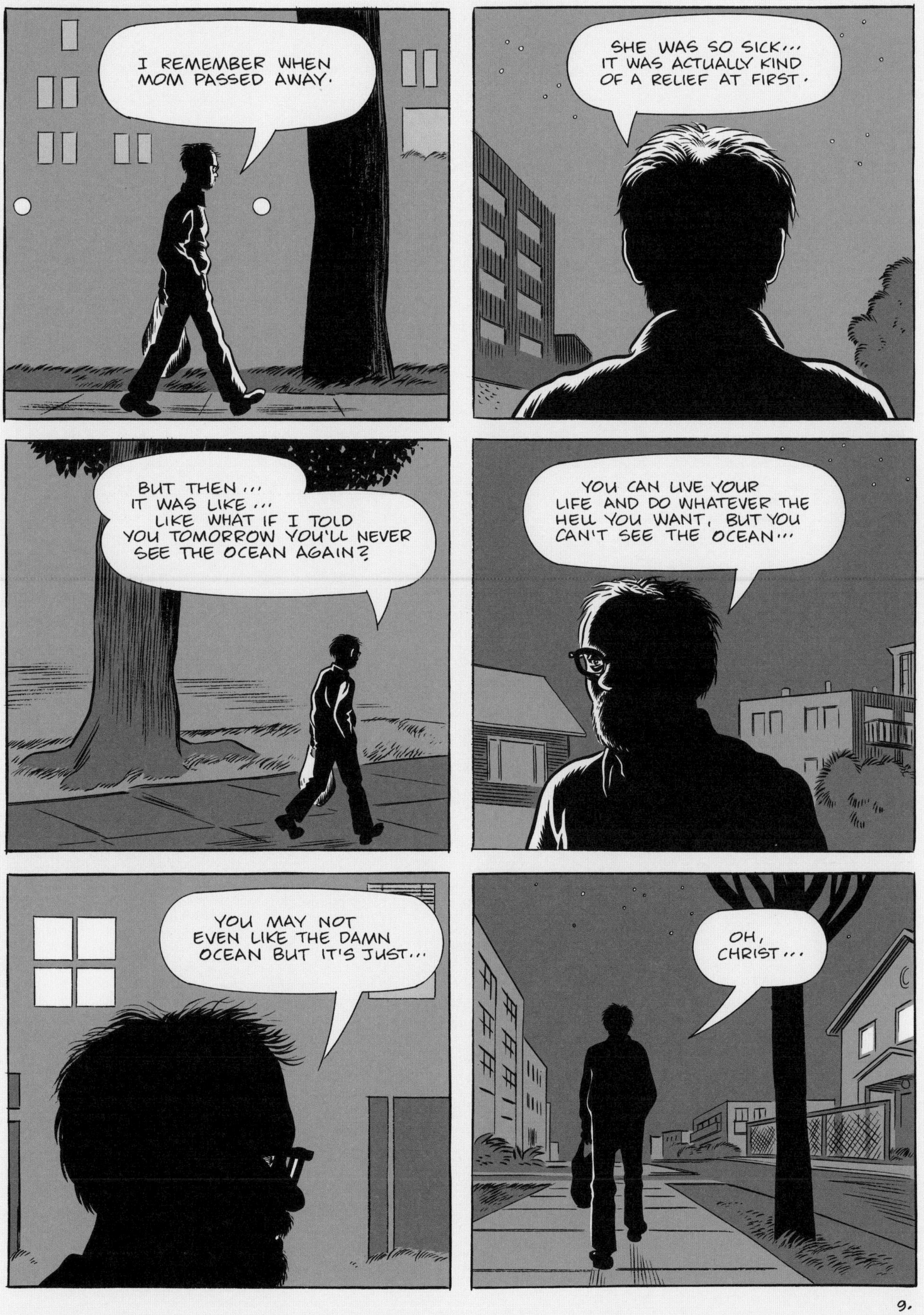
I REMEMBER WHEN MOM PASSED AWAY.
SHE WAS SO SICK... IT WAS ACTUALLY KIND OF A RELIEF AT FIRST.
BUT THEN... IT WAS LIKE... LIKE WHAT IF I TOLD YOU TOMORROW YOU'LL NEVER SEE THE OCEAN AGAIN?
YOU CAN LIVE YOUR LIFE AND DO WHATEVER THE HELL YOU WANT, BUT YOU CAN'T SEE THE OCEAN...
YOU MAY NOT EVEN LIKE THE DAMN OCEAN BUT IT'S JUST...
OH, CHRIST...

CUTE DOG

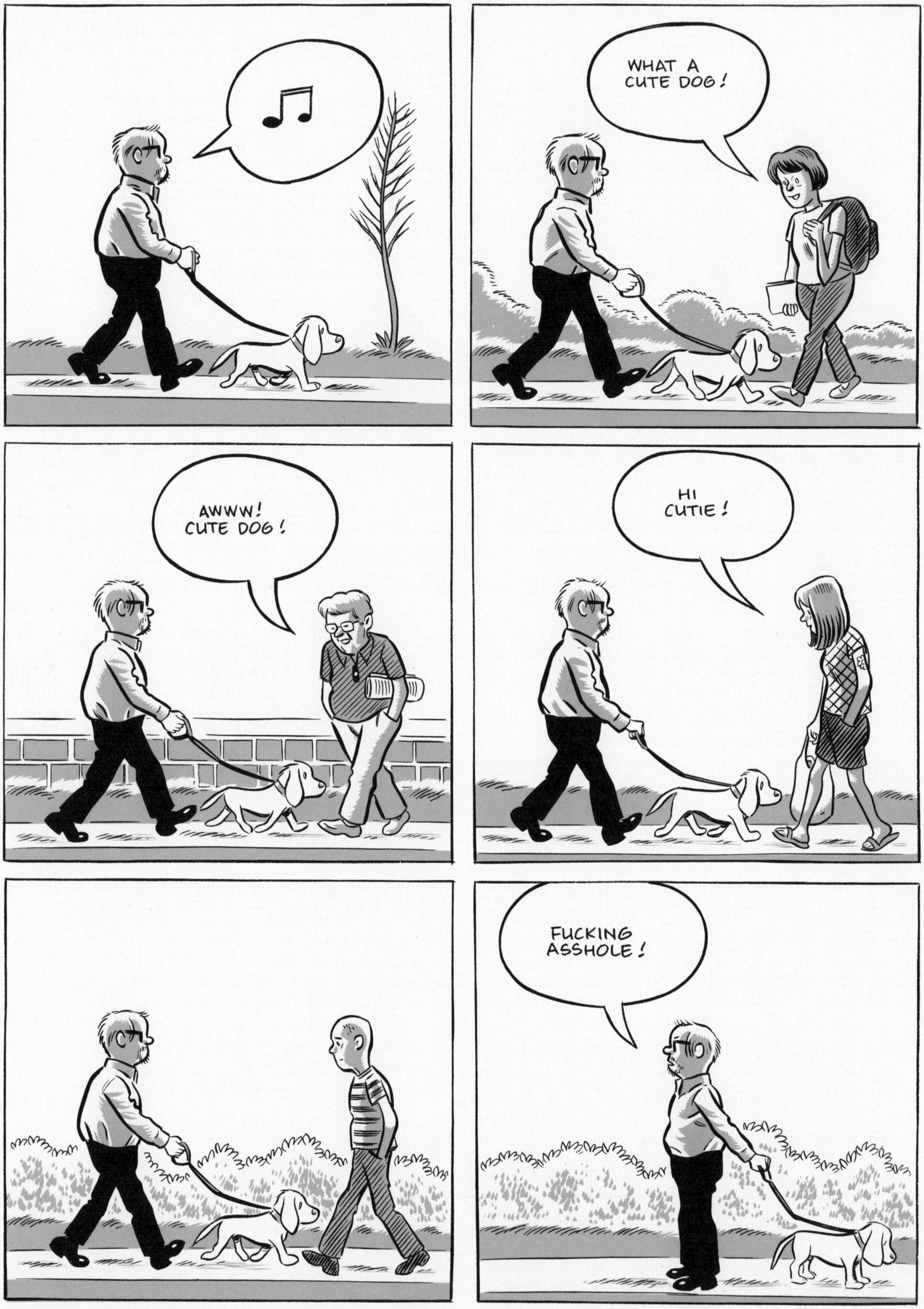

♫
WHAT A CUTE DOG!
AWWW! CUTE DOG!
HI CUTIE!
FUCKING ASSHOLE!

TABLE SHARING

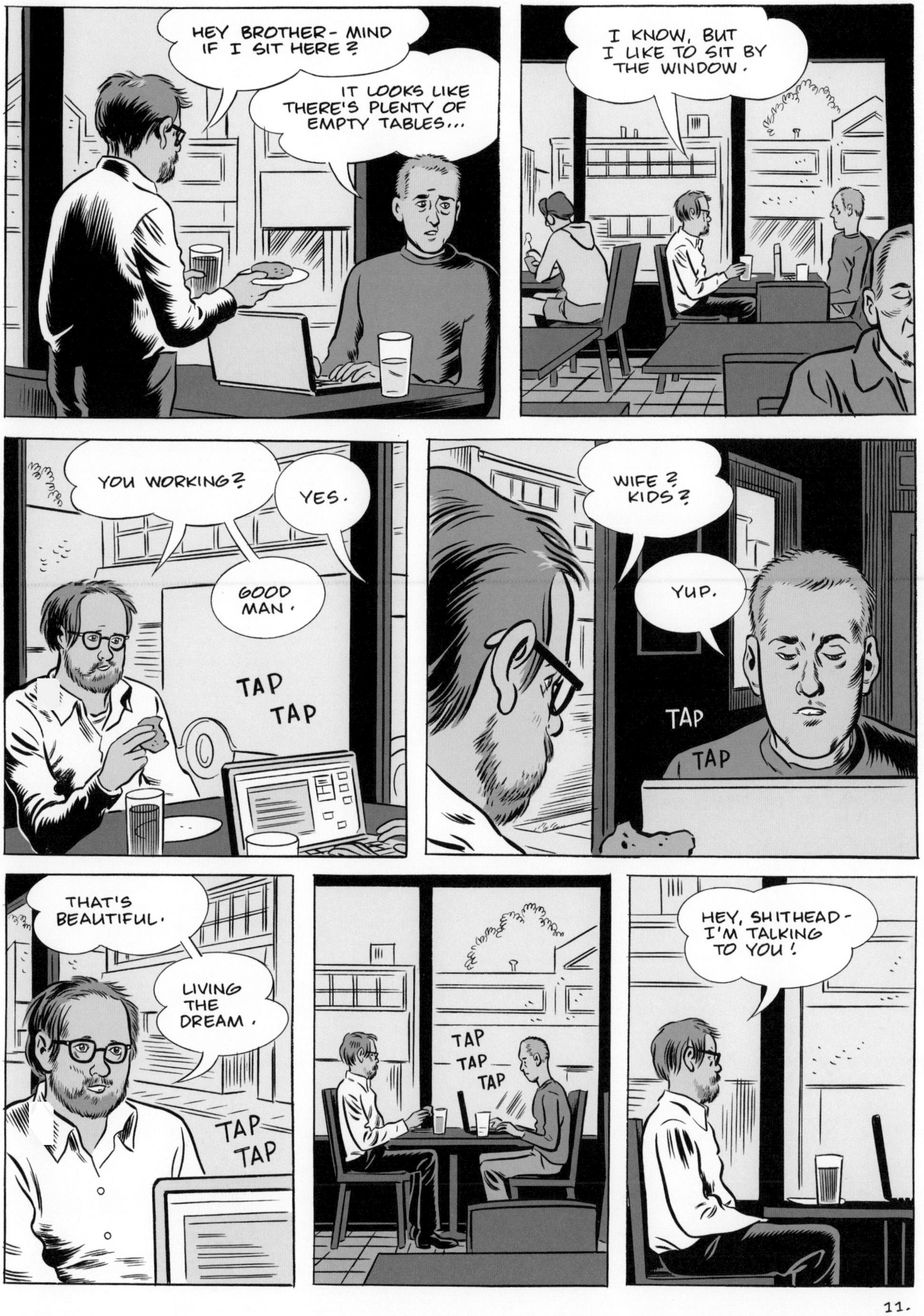
HEY BROTHER- MIND IF I SIT HERE?
IT LOOKS LIKE THERE'S PLENTY OF EMPTY TABLES...
I KNOW, BUT I LIKE TO SIT BY THE WINDOW.
YOU WORKING?
YES.
GOOD MAN.
TAP TAP
WIFE? KIDS?
YUP.
TAP TAP
THAT'S BEAUTIFUL.
LIVING THE DREAM.
TAP TAP
TAP TAP TAP
HEY, SHITHEAD- I'M TALKING TO YOU!

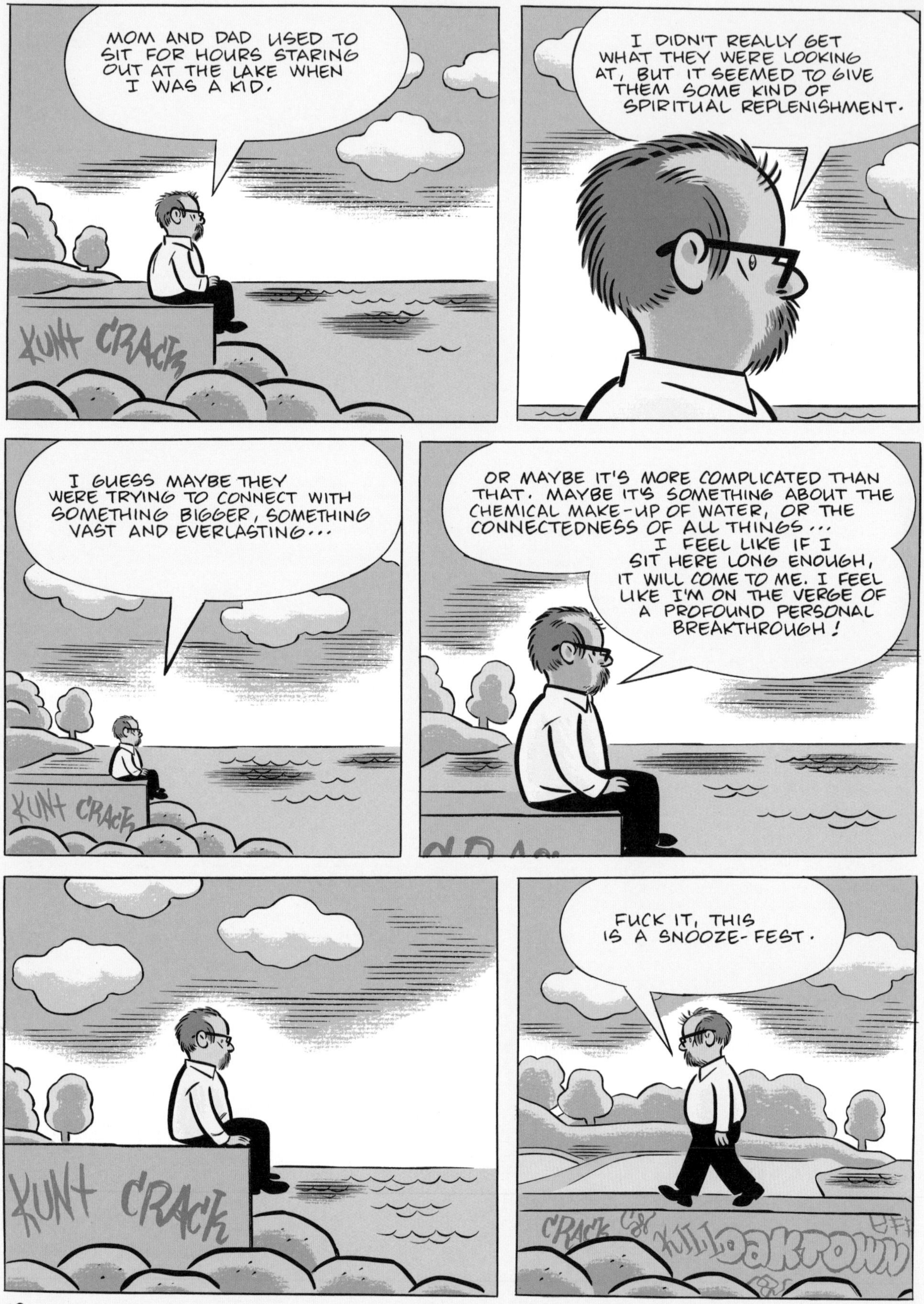
MOM AND DAD USED TO SIT FOR HOURS STARING OUT AT THE LAKE WHEN I WAS A KID.
KUNT CRACK
I DIDN'T REALLY GET WHAT THEY WERE LOOKING AT, BUT IT SEEMED TO GIVE THEM SOME KIND OF SPIRITUAL REPLENISHMENT.
I GUESS MAYBE THEY WERE TRYING TO CONNECT WITH SOMETHING BIGGER, SOMETHING VAST AND EVERLASTING...
KUNT CRACK
OR MAYBE IT'S MORE COMPLICATED THAN THAT. MAYBE IT'S SOMETHING ABOUT THE CHEMICAL MAKE-UP OF WATER, OR THE CONNECTEDNESS OF ALL THINGS...
I FEEL LIKE IF I SIT HERE LONG ENOUGH, IT WILL COME TO ME. I FEEL LIKE I'M ON THE VERGE OF A PROFOUND PERSONAL BREAKTHROUGH!
KUNT CRACK
FUCK IT, THIS IS A SNOOZE-FEST.
CRACK
KILL
OAKTOWN

MARRIAGE

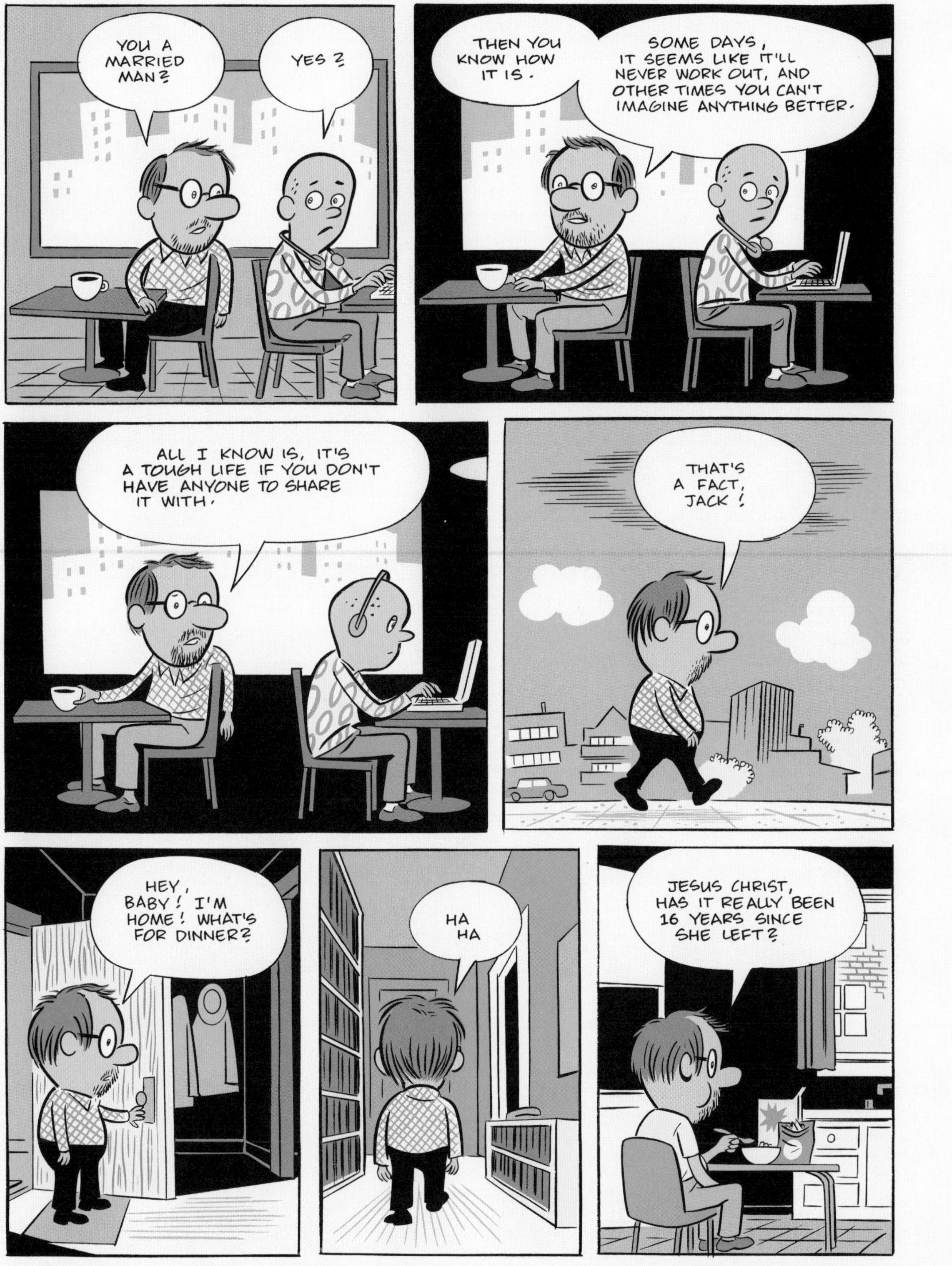

YOU A MARRIED MAN?
YES ?
THEN YOU KNOW HOW IT IS.
SOME DAYS, IT SEEMS LIKE IT'LL NEVER WORK OUT, AND OTHER TIMES YOU CAN'T IMAGINE ANYTHING BETTER.
ALL I KNOW IS, IT'S A TOUGH LIFE IF YOU DON'T HAVE ANYONE TO SHARE IT WITH.
THAT'S A FACT, JACK!
HEY, BABY! I'M HOME! WHAT'S FOR DINNER?
HA HA
JESUS CHRIST, HAS IT REALLY BEEN 16 YEARS SINCE SHE LEFT?

POST OFFICE

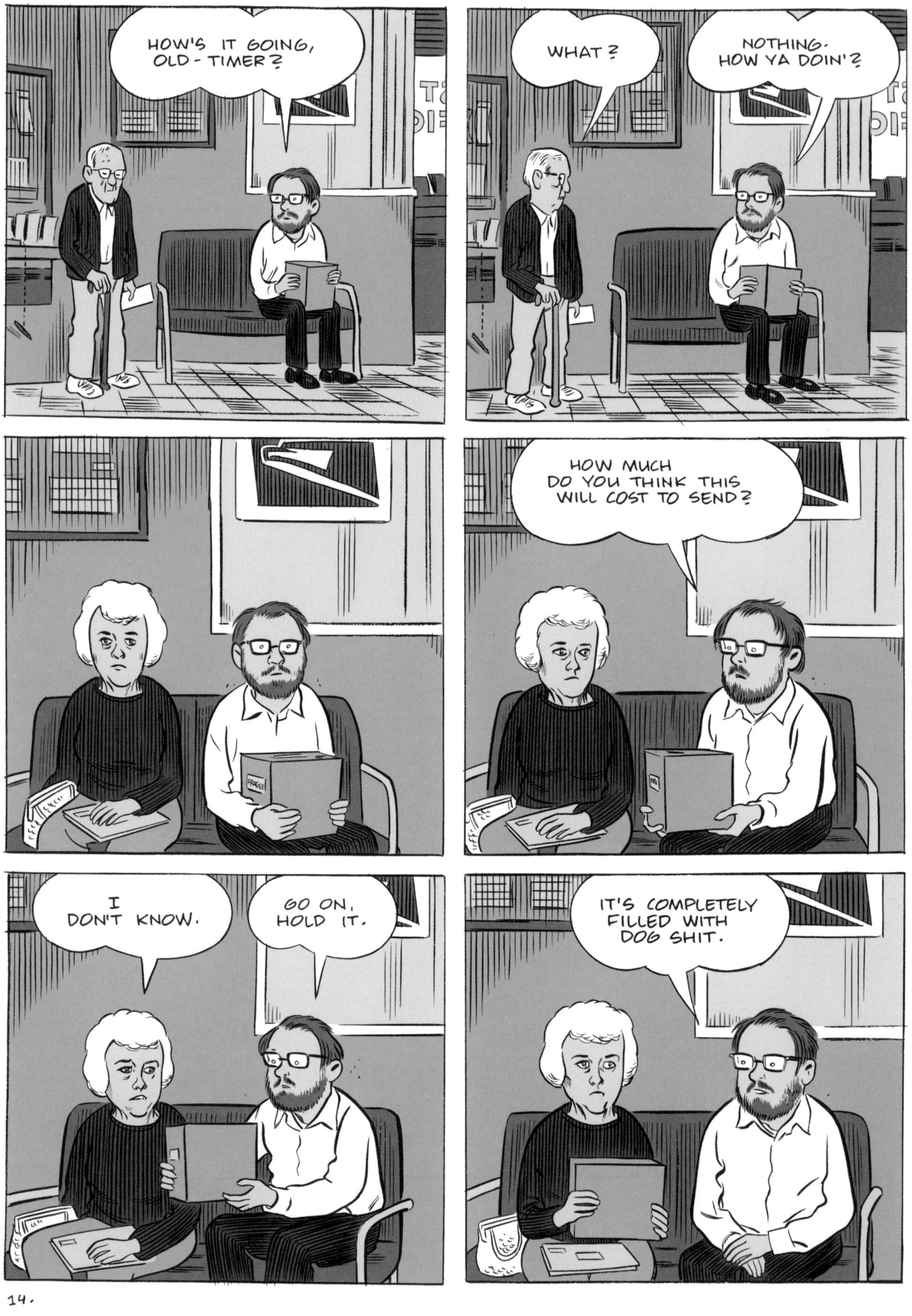
HOW'S IT GOING, OLD-TIMER?
WHAT?
NOTHING. HOW YA DOIN'?
HOW MUCH DO YOU THINK THIS WILL COST TO SEND?
I DON'T KNOW.
GO ON, HOLD IT.
IT'S COMPLETELY FILLED WITH DOG SHIT.

DOG VOICE

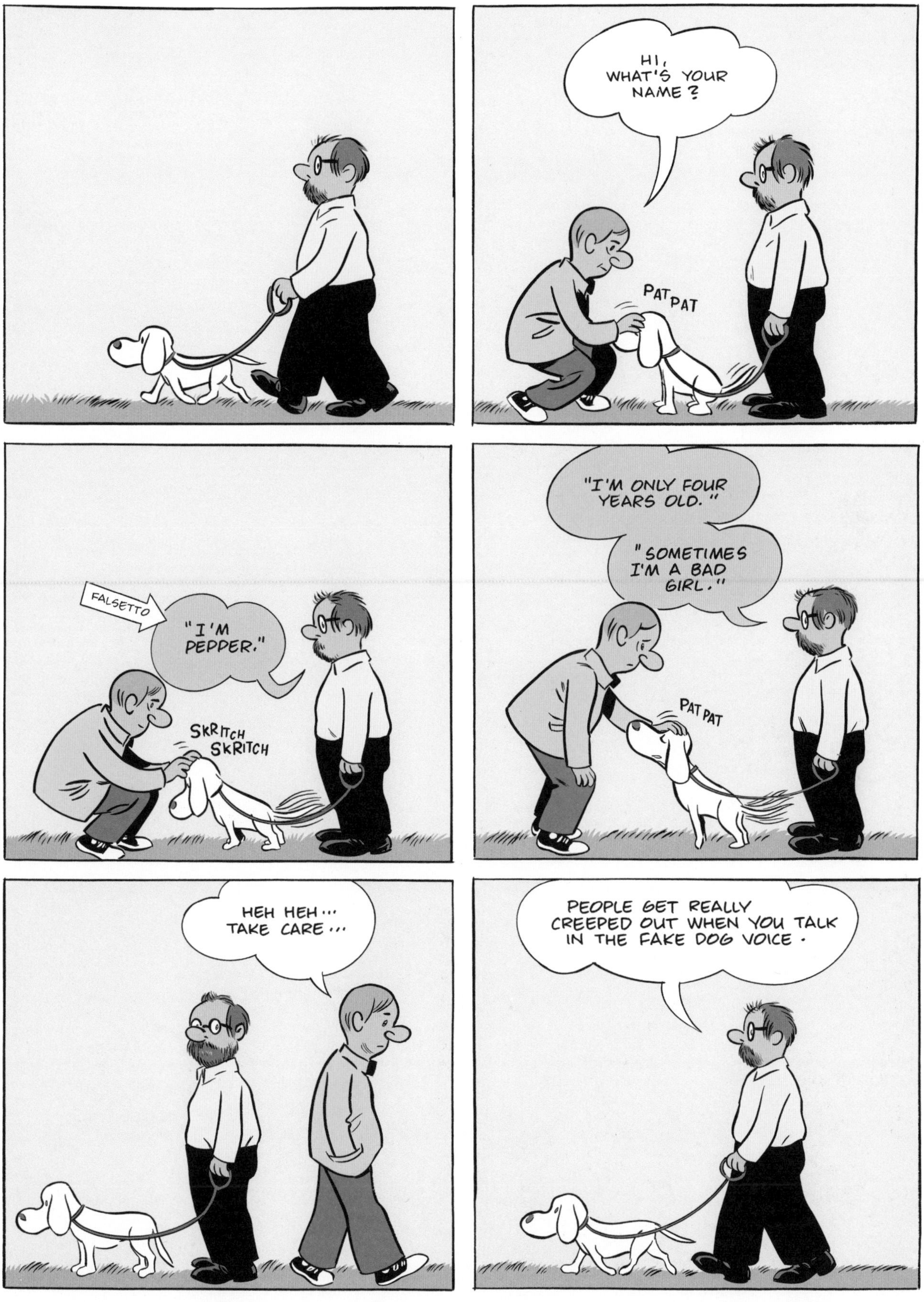
HI, WHAT'S YOUR NAME?
PAT PAT
FALSETTO
"I'M PEPPER."
SKRITCH SKRITCH
"I'M ONLY FOUR YEARS OLD."
"SOMETIMES I'M A BAD GIRL."
PAT PAT
HEH HEH... TAKE CARE...
PEOPLE GET REALLY CREEPED OUT WHEN YOU TALK IN THE FAKE DOG VOICE.

STILL ALIVE

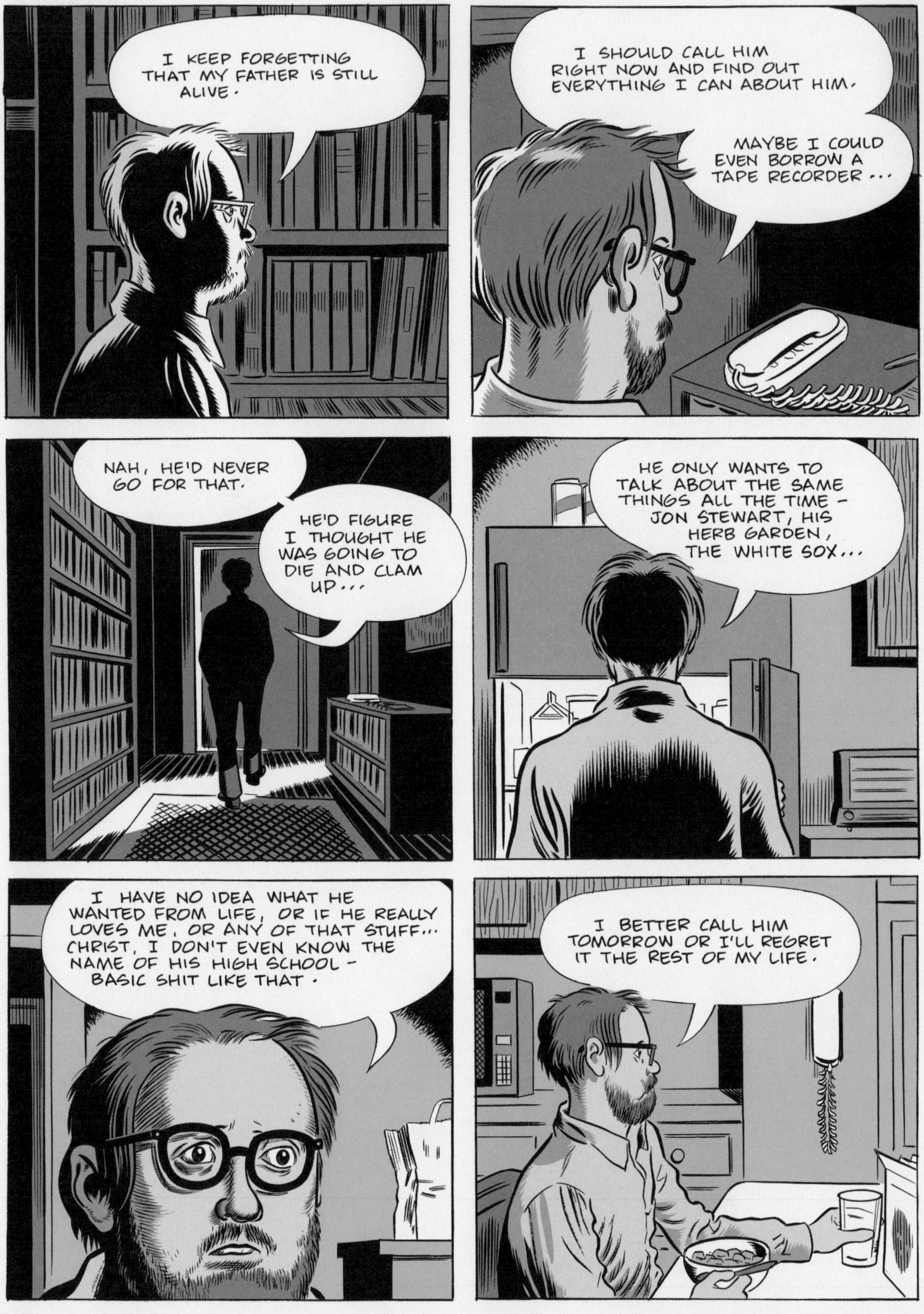
I KEEP FORGETTING THAT MY FATHER IS STILL ALIVE.
I SHOULD CALL HIM RIGHT NOW AND FIND OUT EVERYTHING I CAN ABOUT HIM.
MAYBE I COULD EVEN BORROW A TAPE RECORDER...
NAH, HE'D NEVER GO FOR THAT.
HE'D FIGURE I THOUGHT HE WAS GOING TO DIE AND CLAM UP...
HE ONLY WANTS TO TALK ABOUT THE SAME THINGS ALL THE TIME - JON STEWART, HIS HERB GARDEN, THE WHITE SOX...
I HAVE NO IDEA WHAT HE WANTED FROM LIFE, OR IF HE REALLY LOVES ME, OR ANY OF THAT STUFF... CHRIST, I DON'T EVEN KNOW THE NAME OF HIS HIGH SCHOOL - BASIC SHIT LIKE THAT.
I BETTER CALL HIM TOMORROW OR I'LL REGRET IT THE REST OF MY LIFE.

FAT CHICKS

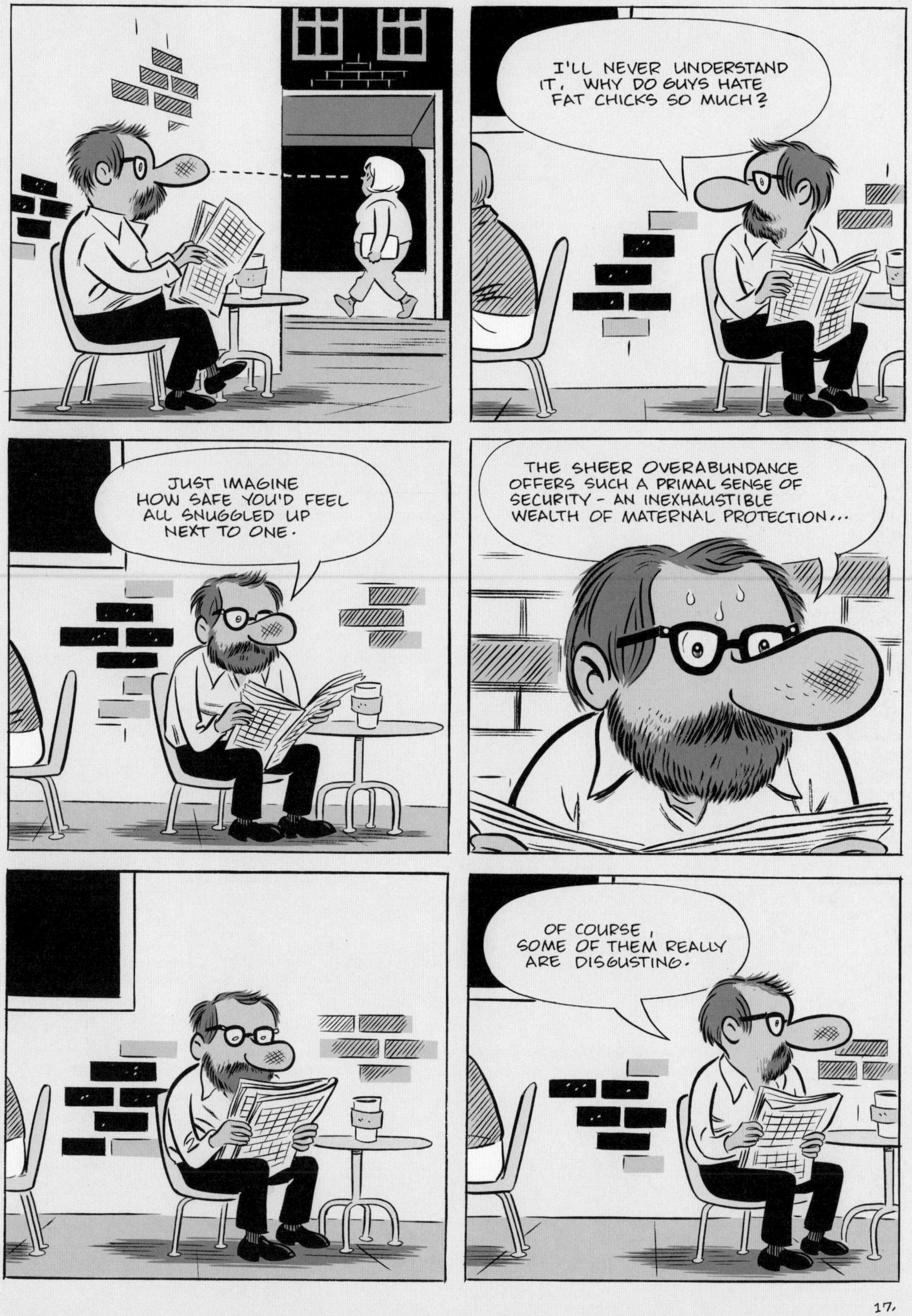
I'LL NEVER UNDERSTAND IT, WHY DO GUYS HATE FAT CHICKS SO MUCH?
JUST IMAGINE HOW SAFE YOU'D FEEL ALL SNUGGLED UP NEXT TO ONE.
THE SHEER OVERABUNDANCE OFFERS SUCH A PRIMAL SENSE OF SECURITY - AN INEXHAUSTIBLE WEALTH OF MATERNAL PROTECTION...
OF COURSE, SOME OF THEM REALLY ARE DISGUSTING.

AGENT OF CHANGE

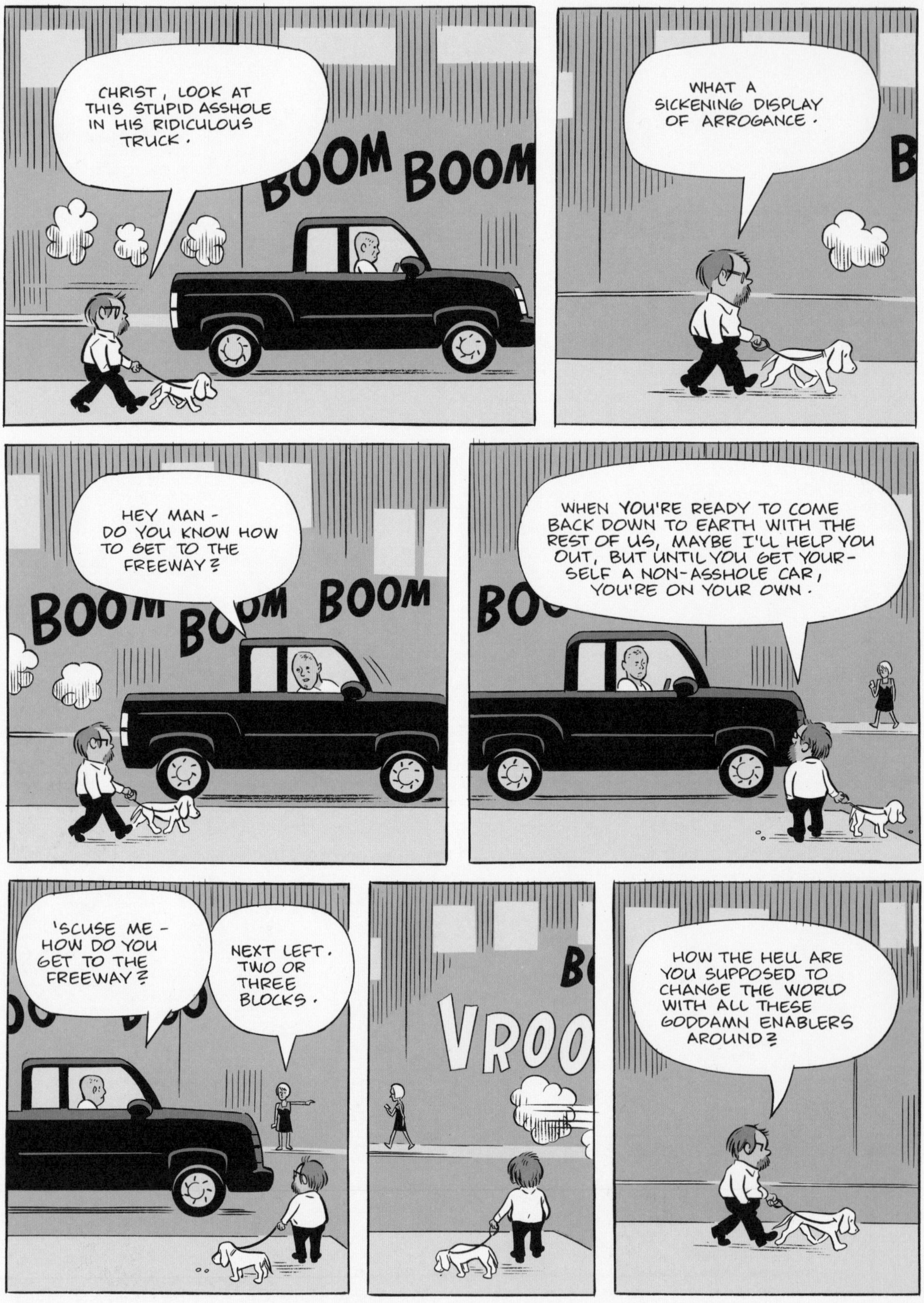

CHRIST, LOOK AT THIS STUPID ASSHOLE IN HIS RIDICULOUS TRUCK.
BOOM BOOM
WHAT A SICKENING DISPLAY OF ARROGANCE.
HEY MAN - DO YOU KNOW HOW TO GET TO THE FREEWAY?
BOOM BOOM
WHEN YOU'RE READY TO COME BACK DOWN TO EARTH WITH THE REST OF US, MAYBE I'LL HELP YOU OUT, BUT UNTIL YOU GET YOURSELF A NON-ASSHOLE CAR, YOU'RE ON YOUR OWN.
'SCUSE ME - HOW DO YOU GET TO THE FREEWAY?
NEXT LEFT. TWO OR THREE BLOCKS.
HOW THE HELL ARE YOU SUPPOSED TO CHANGE THE WORLD WITH ALL THESE GODDAMN ENABLERS AROUND?

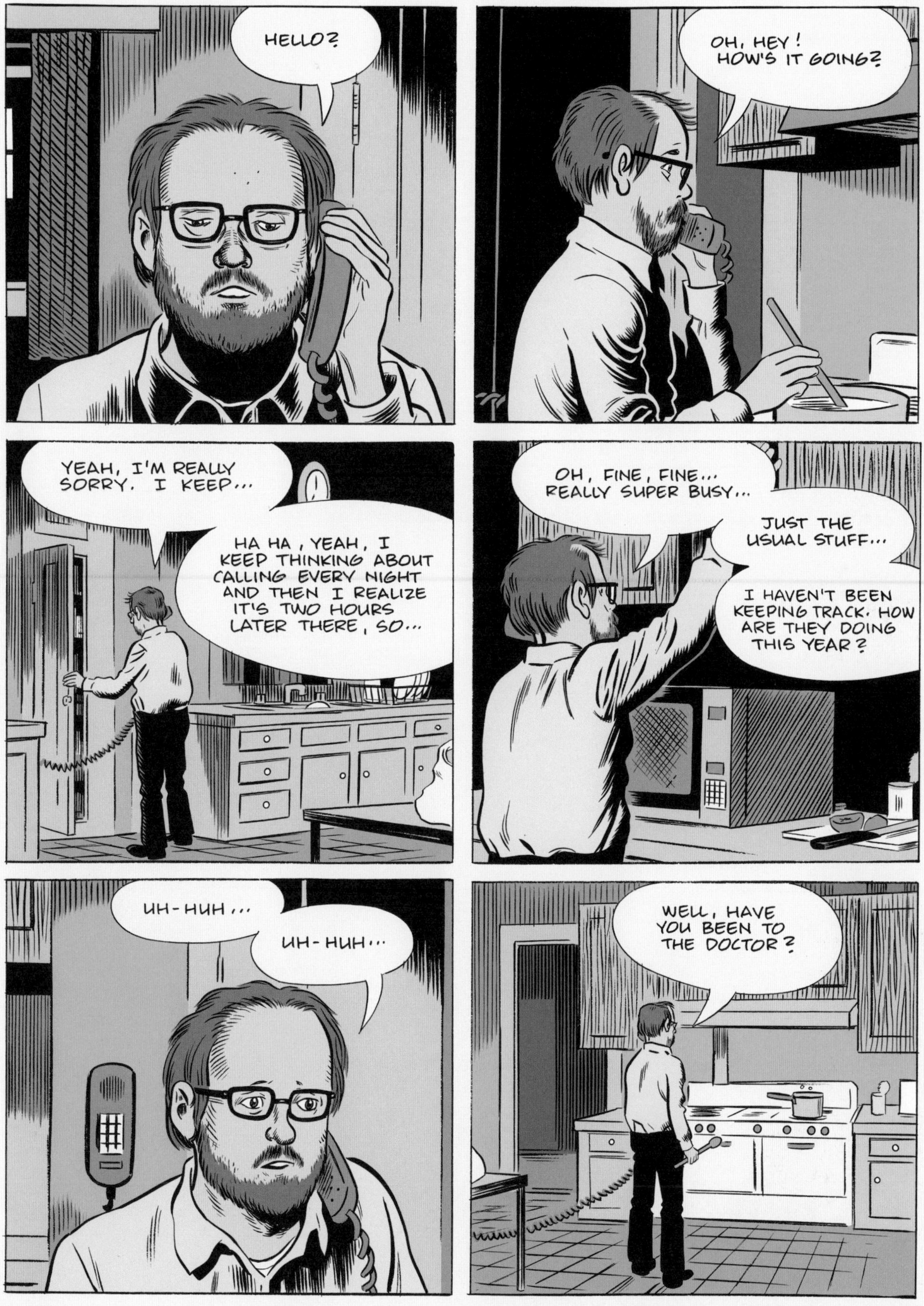
HELLO?
OH, HEY! HOW'S IT GOING?
YEAH, I'M REALLY SORRY. I KEEP...
HA HA, YEAH, I KEEP THINKING ABOUT CALLING EVERY NIGHT AND THEN I REALIZE IT'S TWO HOURS LATER THERE, SO...
OH, FINE, FINE... REALLY SUPER BUSY...
JUST THE USUAL STUFF...
I HAVEN'T BEEN KEEPING TRACK. HOW ARE THEY DOING THIS YEAR?
UH-HUH...
UH-HUH...
WELL, HAVE YOU BEEN TO THE DOCTOR?

DOGSITTER

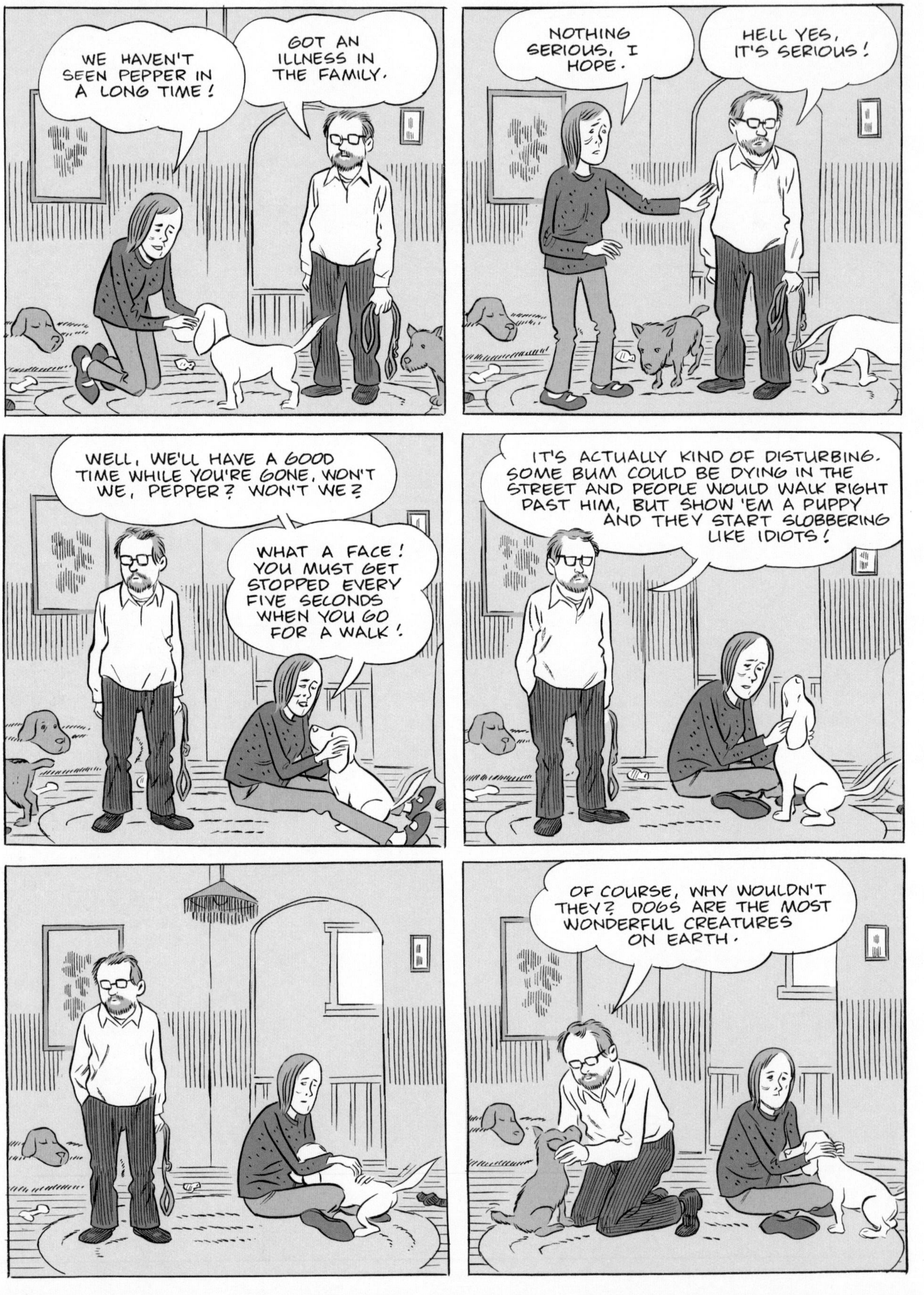
WE HAVEN'T SEEN PEPPER IN A LONG TIME!
GOT AN ILLNESS IN THE FAMILY.
NOTHING SERIOUS, I HOPE.
HELL YES, IT'S SERIOUS!
WELL, WE'LL HAVE A GOOD TIME WHILE YOU'RE GONE, WON'T WE, PEPPER? WON'T WE?
WHAT A FACE! YOU MUST GET STOPPED EVERY FIVE SECONDS WHEN YOU GO FOR A WALK!
IT'S ACTUALLY KIND OF DISTURBING. SOME BUM COULD BE DYING IN THE STREET AND PEOPLE WOULD WALK RIGHT PAST HIM, BUT SHOW 'EM A PUPPY AND THEY START SLOBBERING LIKE IDIOTS!
OF COURSE, WHY WOULDN'T THEY? DOGS ARE THE MOST WONDERFUL CREATURES ON EARTH.

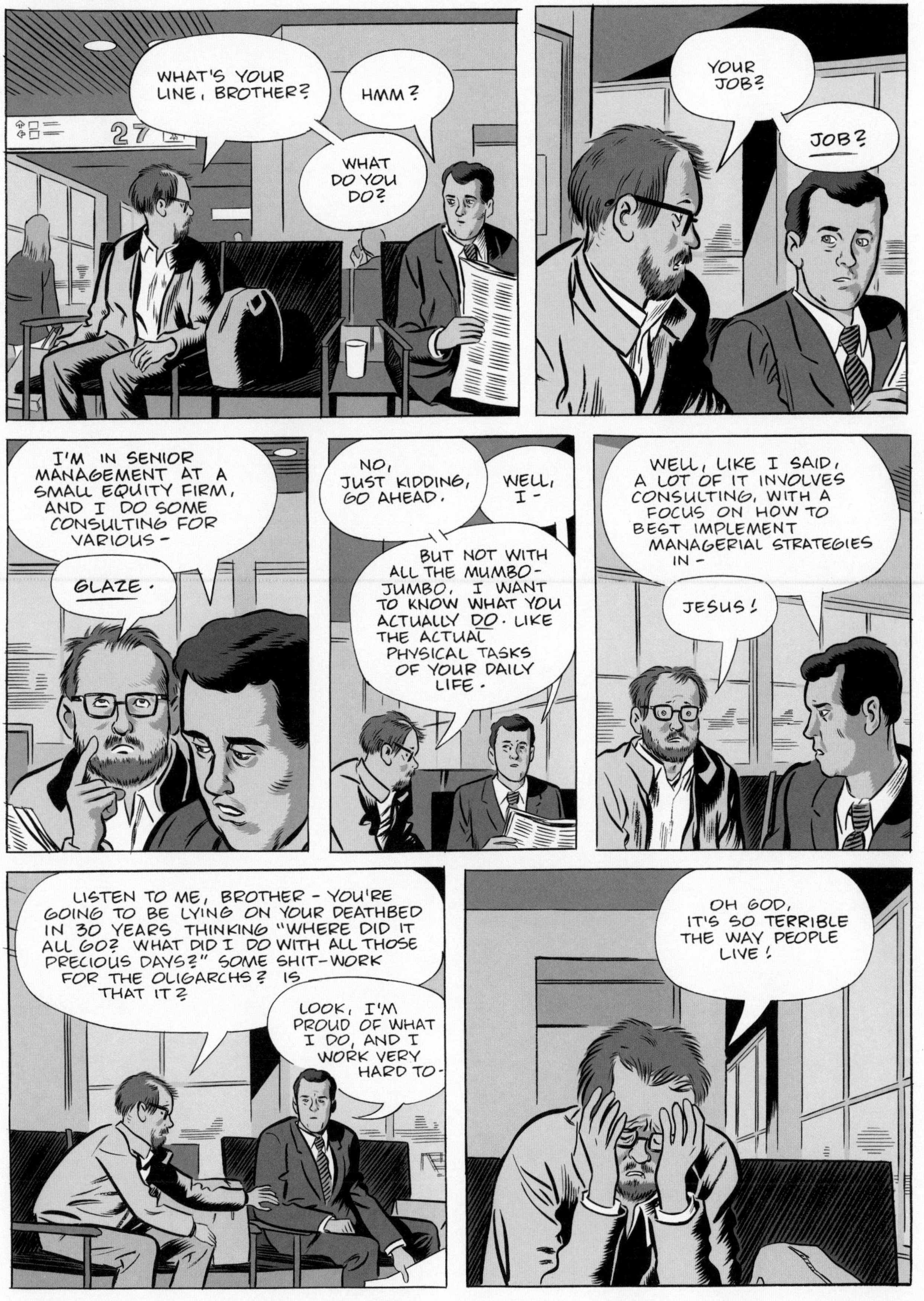
WHAT'S YOUR LINE, BROTHER?
HMM?
WHAT DO YOU DO?
27
YOUR JOB?
JOB?
I'M IN SENIOR MANAGEMENT AT A SMALL EQUITY FIRM, AND I DO SOME CONSULTING FOR VARIOUS -
GLAZE.
NO, JUST KIDDING, GO AHEAD.
WELL, I -
BUT NOT WITH ALL THE MUMBO-JUMBO, I WANT TO KNOW WHAT YOU ACTUALLY DO. LIKE THE ACTUAL PHYSICAL TASKS OF YOUR DAILY LIFE.
WELL, LIKE I SAID, A LOT OF IT INVOLVES CONSULTING, WITH A FOCUS ON HOW TO BEST IMPLEMENT MANAGERIAL STRATEGIES IN -
JESUS!
LISTEN TO ME, BROTHER - YOU'RE GOING TO BE LYING ON YOUR DEATHBED IN 30 YEARS THINKING "WHERE DID IT ALL GO? WHAT DID I DO WITH ALL THOSE PRECIOUS DAYS?" SOME SHIT-WORK FOR THE OLIGARCHS? IS THAT IT?
LOOK, I'M PROUD OF WHAT I DO, AND I WORK VERY HARD TO-
OH GOD, IT'S SO TERRIBLE THE WAY PEOPLE LIVE!

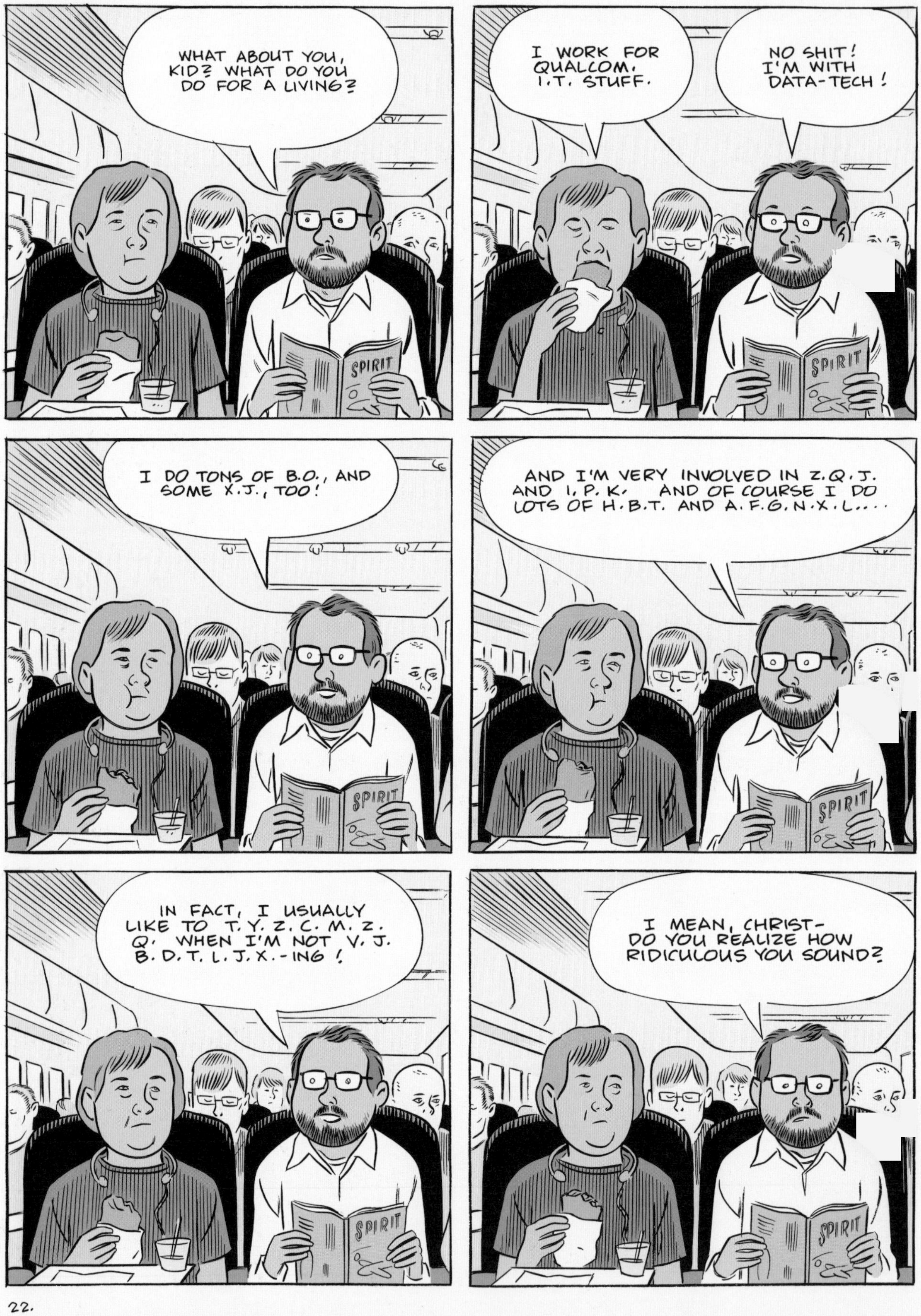
WHAT ABOUT YOU, KID? WHAT DO YOU DO FOR A LIVING?
I WORK FOR QUALCOM. I.T. STUFF.
NO SHIT! I'M WITH DATA-TECH!
I DO TONS OF B.O., AND SOME X.J., TOO!
AND I'M VERY INVOLVED IN Z.Q.J. AND I.P.K. AND OF COURSE I DO LOTS OF H.B.T. AND A.F.G.N.X.L....
IN FACT, I USUALLY LIKE TO T.Y.Z.C.M.Z.Q. WHEN I'M NOT V.J.B.D.T.L.J.X.-ING!
SPIRIT
I MEAN, CHRIST- DO YOU REALIZE HOW RIDICULOUS YOU SOUND?

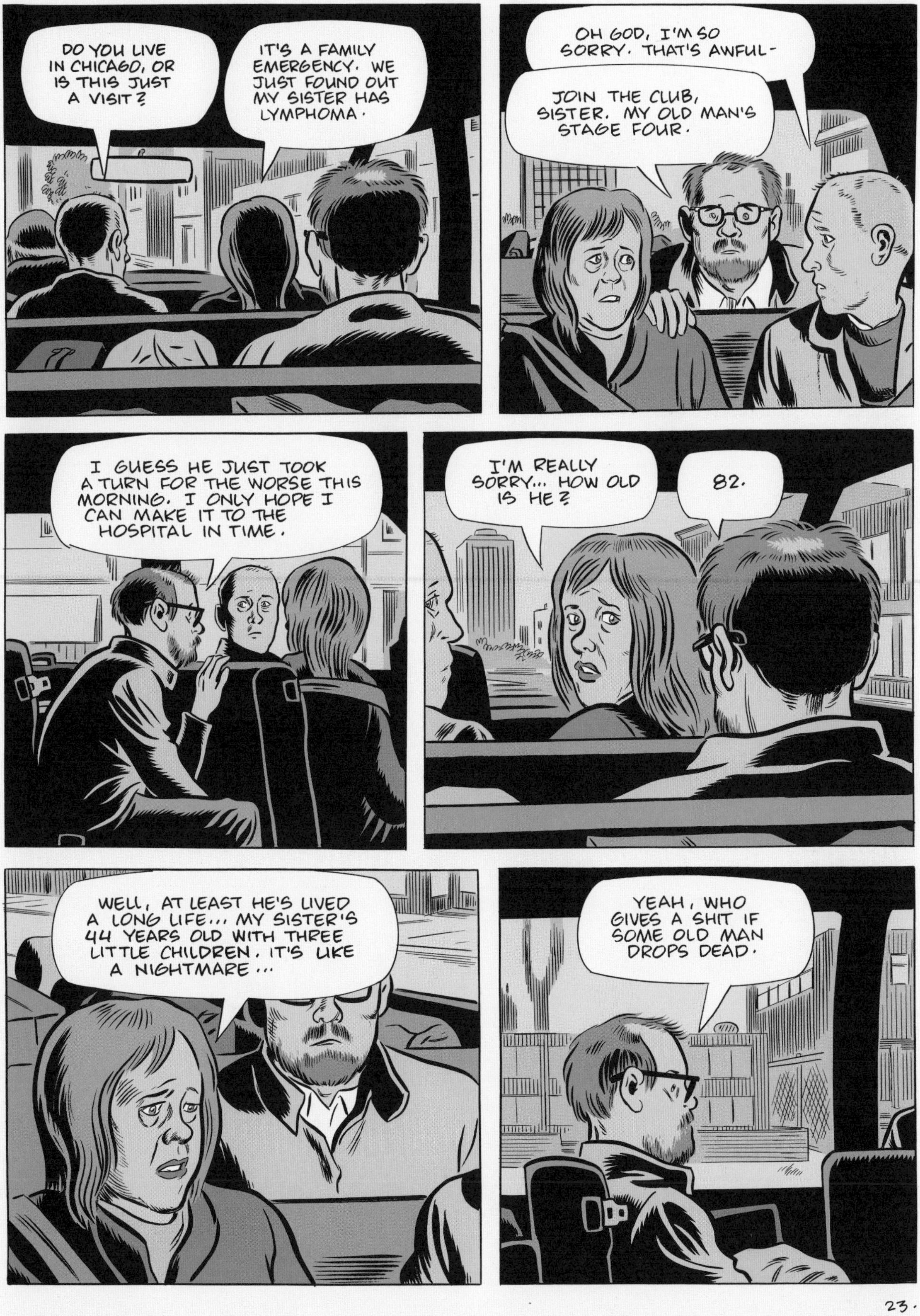
DO YOU LIVE IN CHICAGO, OR IS THIS JUST A VISIT?
IT'S A FAMILY EMERGENCY. WE JUST FOUND OUT MY SISTER HAS LYMPHOMA.
OH GOD, I'M SO SORRY. THAT'S AWFUL-
JOIN THE CLUB, SISTER. MY OLD MAN'S STAGE FOUR.
I GUESS HE JUST TOOK A TURN FOR THE WORSE THIS MORNING. I ONLY HOPE I CAN MAKE IT TO THE HOSPITAL IN TIME.
I'M REALLY SORRY... HOW OLD IS HE?
82.
WELL, AT LEAST HE'S LIVED A LONG LIFE... MY SISTER'S 44 YEARS OLD WITH THREE LITTLE CHILDREN. IT'S LIKE A NIGHTMARE...
YEAH, WHO GIVES A SHIT IF SOME OLD MAN DROPS DEAD.

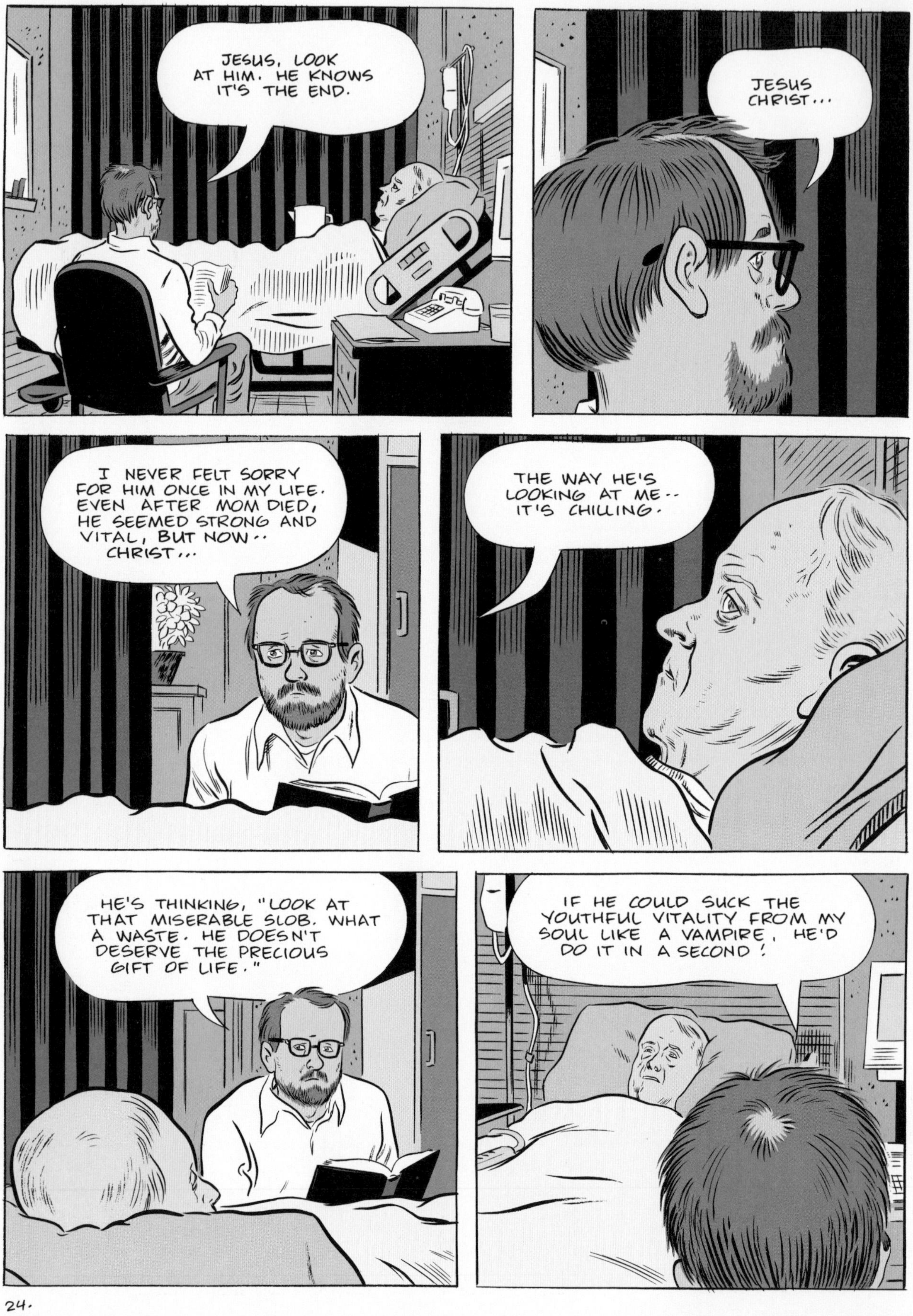
JESUS, LOOK AT HIM. HE KNOWS IT'S THE END.
JESUS CHRIST...
I NEVER FELT SORRY FOR HIM ONCE IN MY LIFE. EVEN AFTER MOM DIED, HE SEEMED STRONG AND VITAL, BUT NOW.. CHRIST...
THE WAY HE'S LOOKING AT ME.. IT'S CHILLING.
HE'S THINKING, "LOOK AT THAT MISERABLE SLOB. WHAT A WASTE. HE DOESN'T DESERVE THE PRECIOUS GIFT OF LIFE."
IF HE COULD SUCK THE YOUTHFUL VITALITY FROM MY SOUL LIKE A VAMPIRE, HE'D DO IT IN A SECOND!

NURSE HEATH

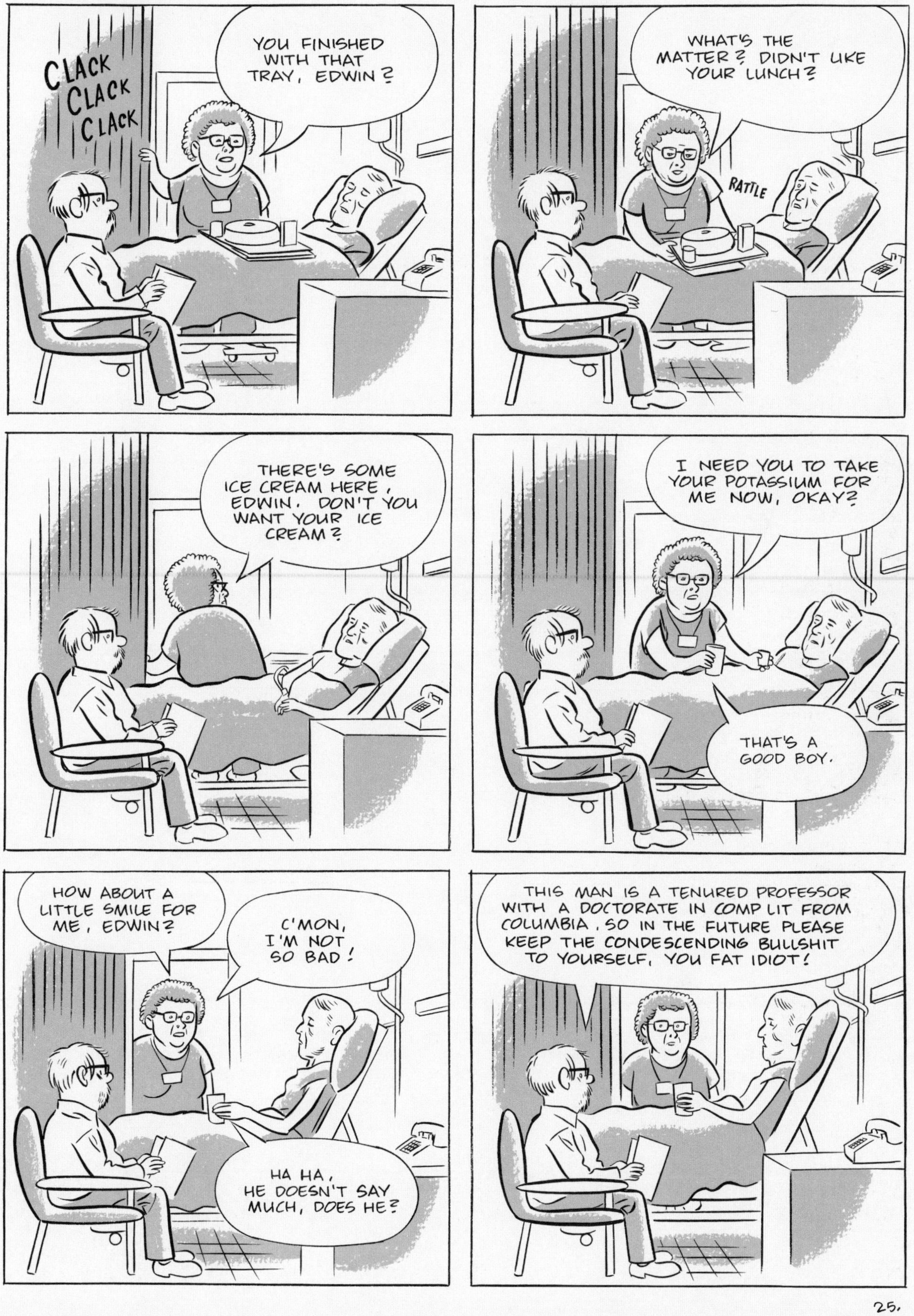

CLACK CLACK CLACK
YOU FINISHED WITH THAT TRAY, EDWIN?
WHAT'S THE MATTER? DIDN'T LIKE YOUR LUNCH?
RATTLE
THERE'S SOME ICE CREAM HERE, EDWIN. DON'T YOU WANT YOUR ICE CREAM?
I NEED YOU TO TAKE YOUR POTASSIUM FOR ME NOW, OKAY?
THAT'S A GOOD BOY.
HOW ABOUT A LITTLE SMILE FOR ME, EDWIN?
C'MON, I'M NOT SO BAD!
HA HA, HE DOESN'T SAY MUCH, DOES HE?
THIS MAN IS A TENURED PROFESSOR WITH A DOCTORATE IN COMP LIT FROM COLUMBIA, SO IN THE FUTURE PLEASE KEEP THE CONDESCENDING BULLSHIT TO YOURSELF, YOU FAT IDIOT!

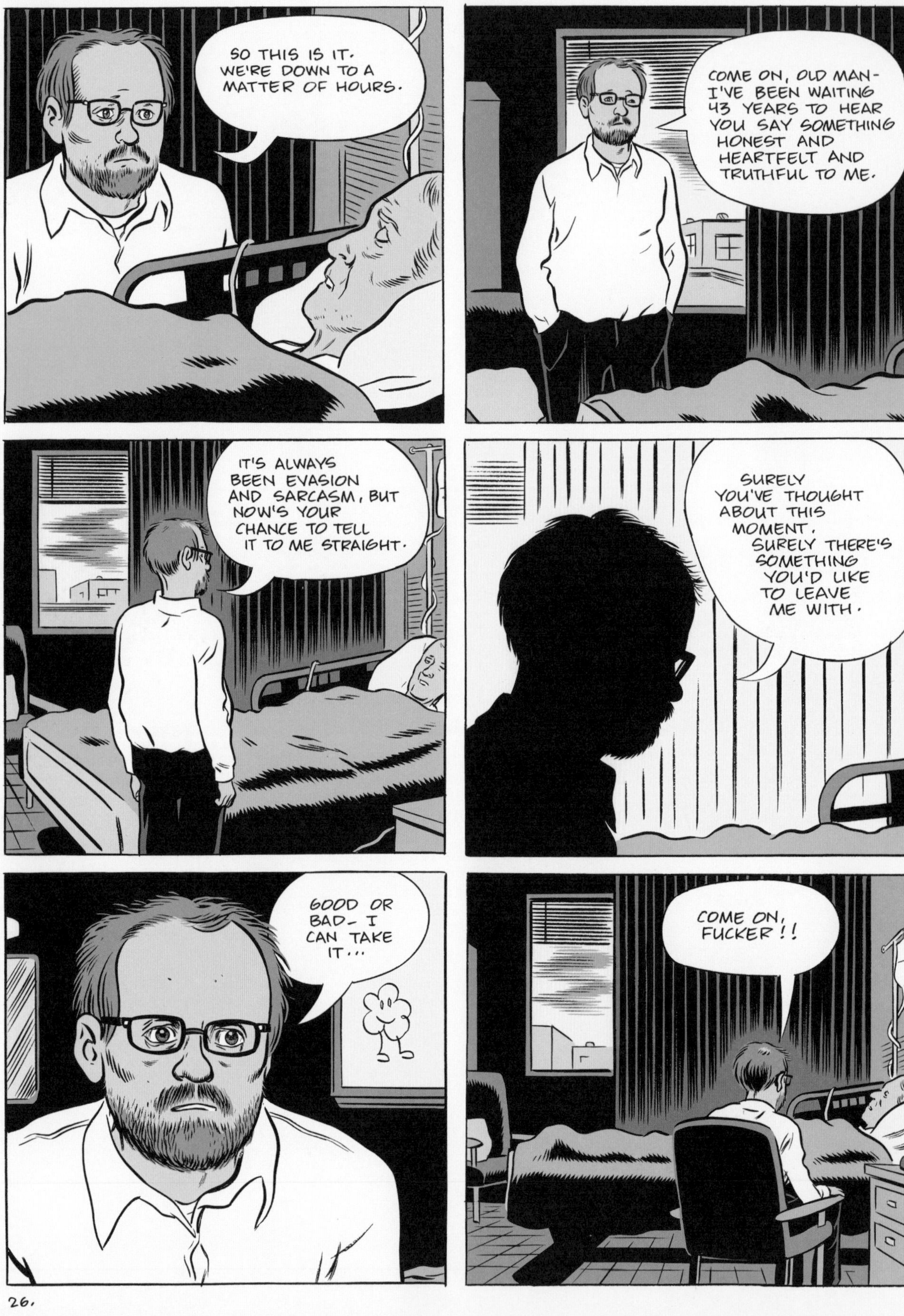
SO THIS IS IT. WE'RE DOWN TO A MATTER OF HOURS.
COME ON, OLD MAN- I'VE BEEN WAITING 43 YEARS TO HEAR YOU SAY SOMETHING HONEST AND HEARTFELT AND TRUTHFUL TO ME.
IT'S ALWAYS BEEN EVASION AND SARCASM, BUT NOW'S YOUR CHANCE TO TELL IT TO ME STRAIGHT.
SURELY YOU'VE THOUGHT ABOUT THIS MOMENT. SURELY THERE'S SOMETHING YOU'D LIKE TO LEAVE ME WITH.
GOOD OR BAD- I CAN TAKE IT...
COME ON, FUCKER!!

THE OLD NEIGHBORHOOD

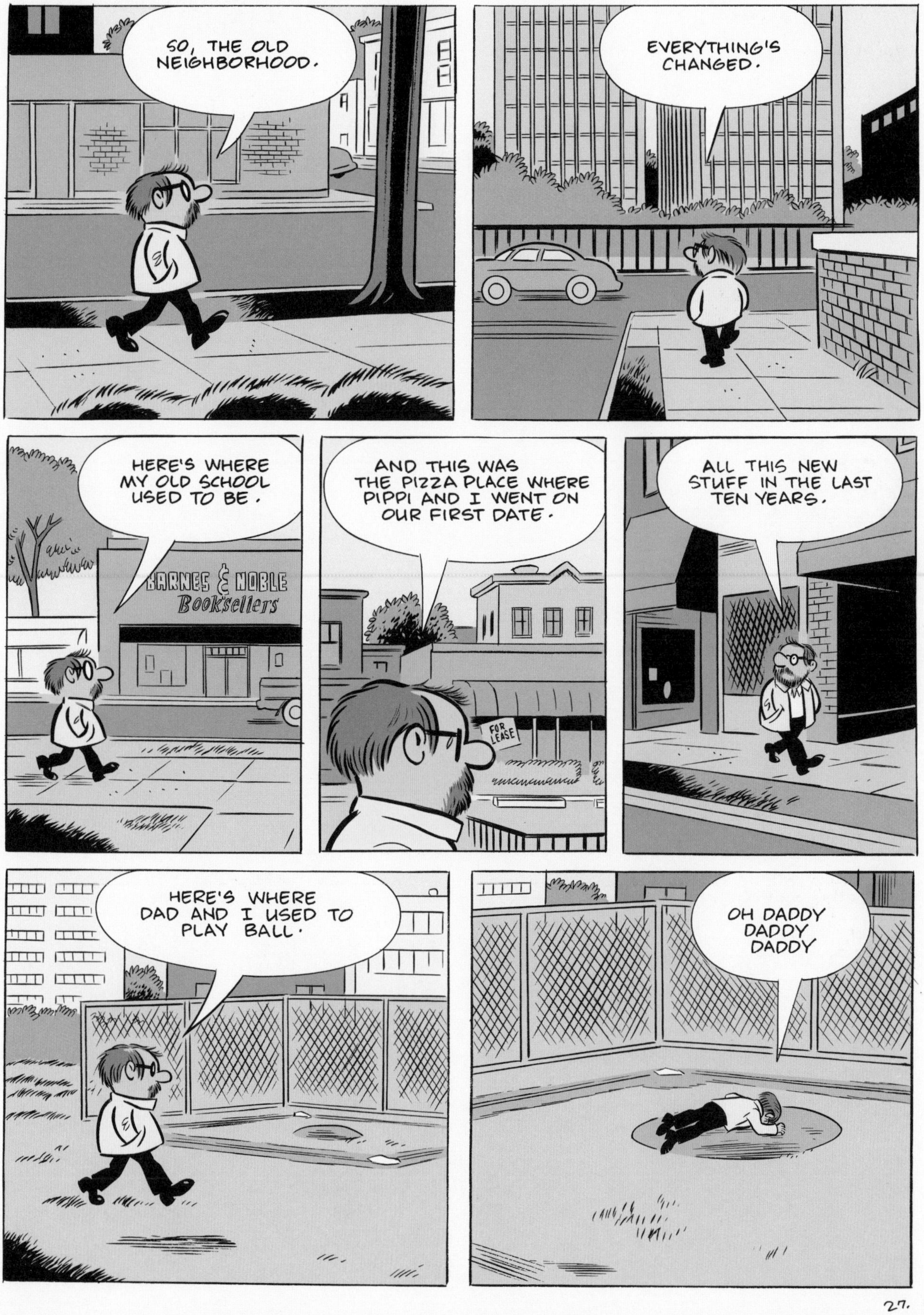
SO, THE OLD NEIGHBORHOOD.
EVERYTHING'S CHANGED.
HERE'S WHERE MY OLD SCHOOL USED TO BE.
BARNES & NOBLE Booksellers
AND THIS WAS THE PIZZA PLACE WHERE PIPPI AND I WENT ON OUR FIRST DATE.
FOR LEASE
ALL THIS NEW STUFF IN THE LAST TEN YEARS.
HERE'S WHERE DAD AND I USED TO PLAY BALL.
OH DADDY DADDY DADDY

ALL ALONE

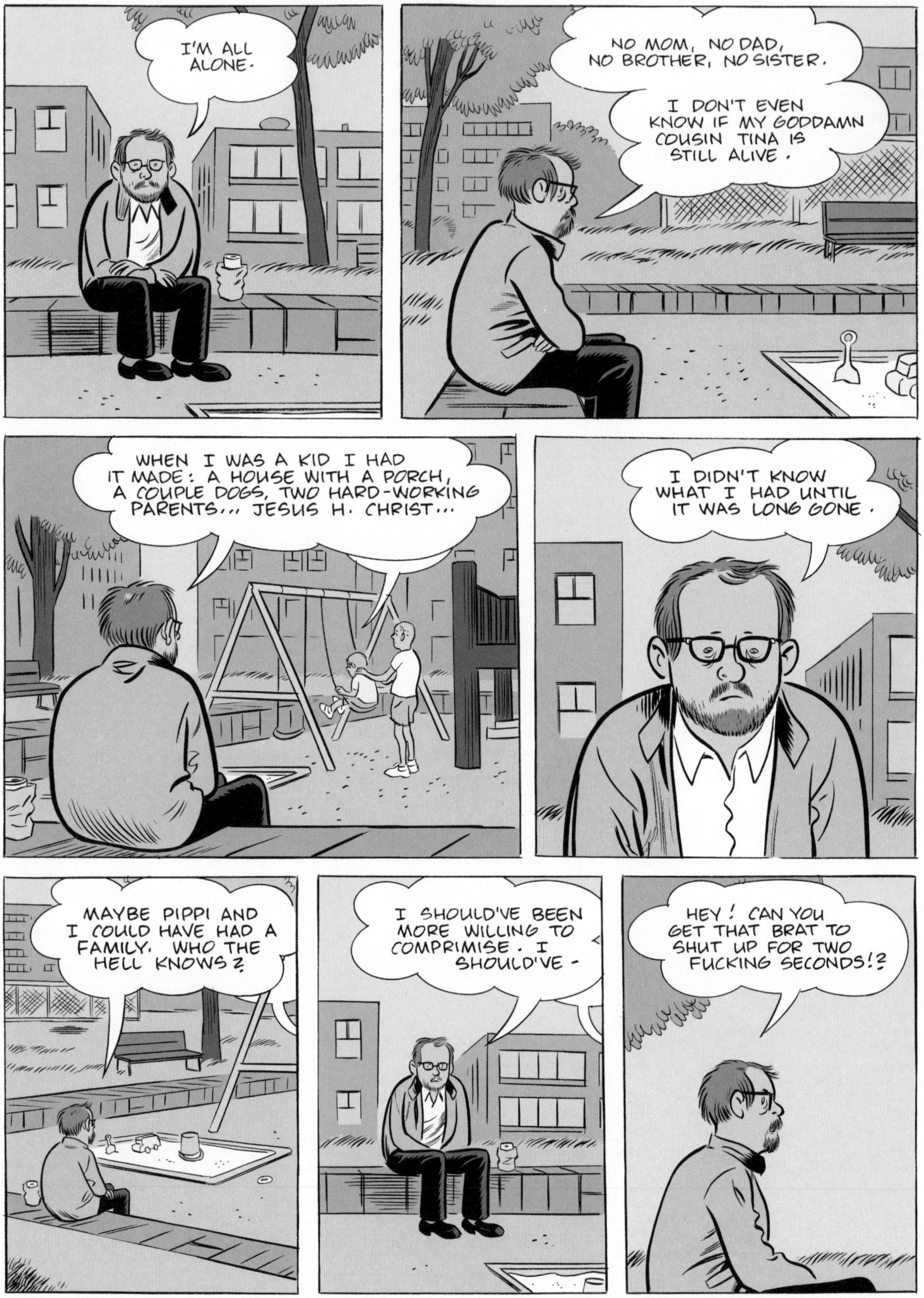
I'M ALL ALONE.
NO MOM, NO DAD, NO BROTHER, NO SISTER.
I DON'T EVEN KNOW IF MY GODDAMN COUSIN TINA IS STILL ALIVE.
WHEN I WAS A KID I HAD IT MADE: A HOUSE WITH A PORCH, A COUPLE DOGS, TWO HARD-WORKING PARENTS... JESUS H. CHRIST...
I DIDN'T KNOW WHAT I HAD UNTIL IT WAS LONG GONE.
MAYBE PIPPI AND I COULD HAVE HAD A FAMILY. WHO THE HELL KNOWS?
I SHOULD'VE BEEN MORE WILLING TO COMPRIMISE. I SHOULD'VE -
HEY! CAN YOU GET THAT BRAT TO SHUT UP FOR TWO FUCKING SECONDS!?

OUT OF THE BLUE

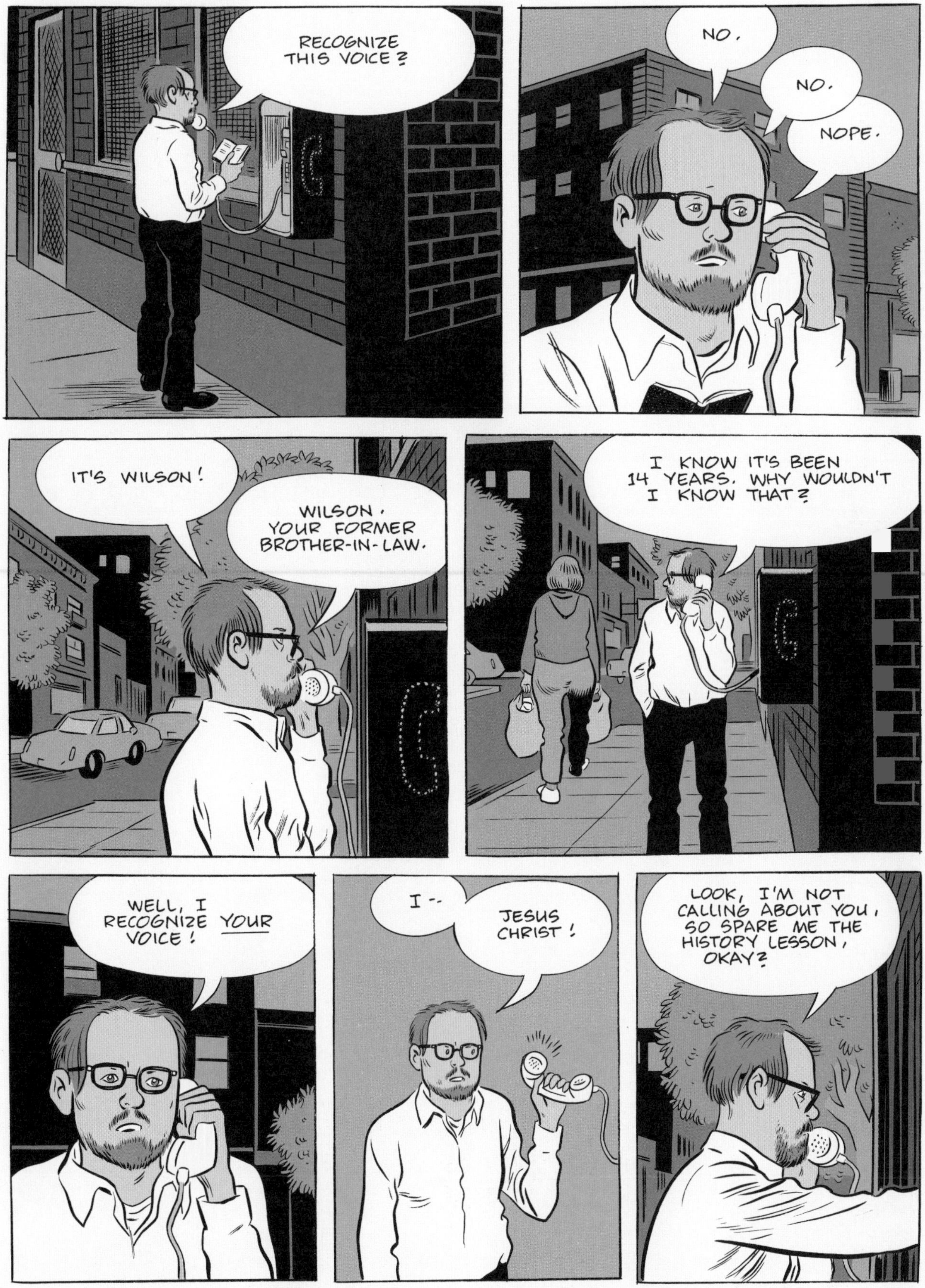

RECOGNIZE THIS VOICE?
NO.
NO.
NOPE.
IT'S WILSON!
WILSON, YOUR FORMER BROTHER-IN-LAW.
I KNOW IT'S BEEN 14 YEARS. WHY WOULDN'T I KNOW THAT?
WELL, I RECOGNIZE YOUR VOICE!
I --
JESUS CHRIST!
LOOK, I'M NOT CALLING ABOUT YOU, SO SPARE ME THE HISTORY LESSON, OKAY?

LONG DISTANCE

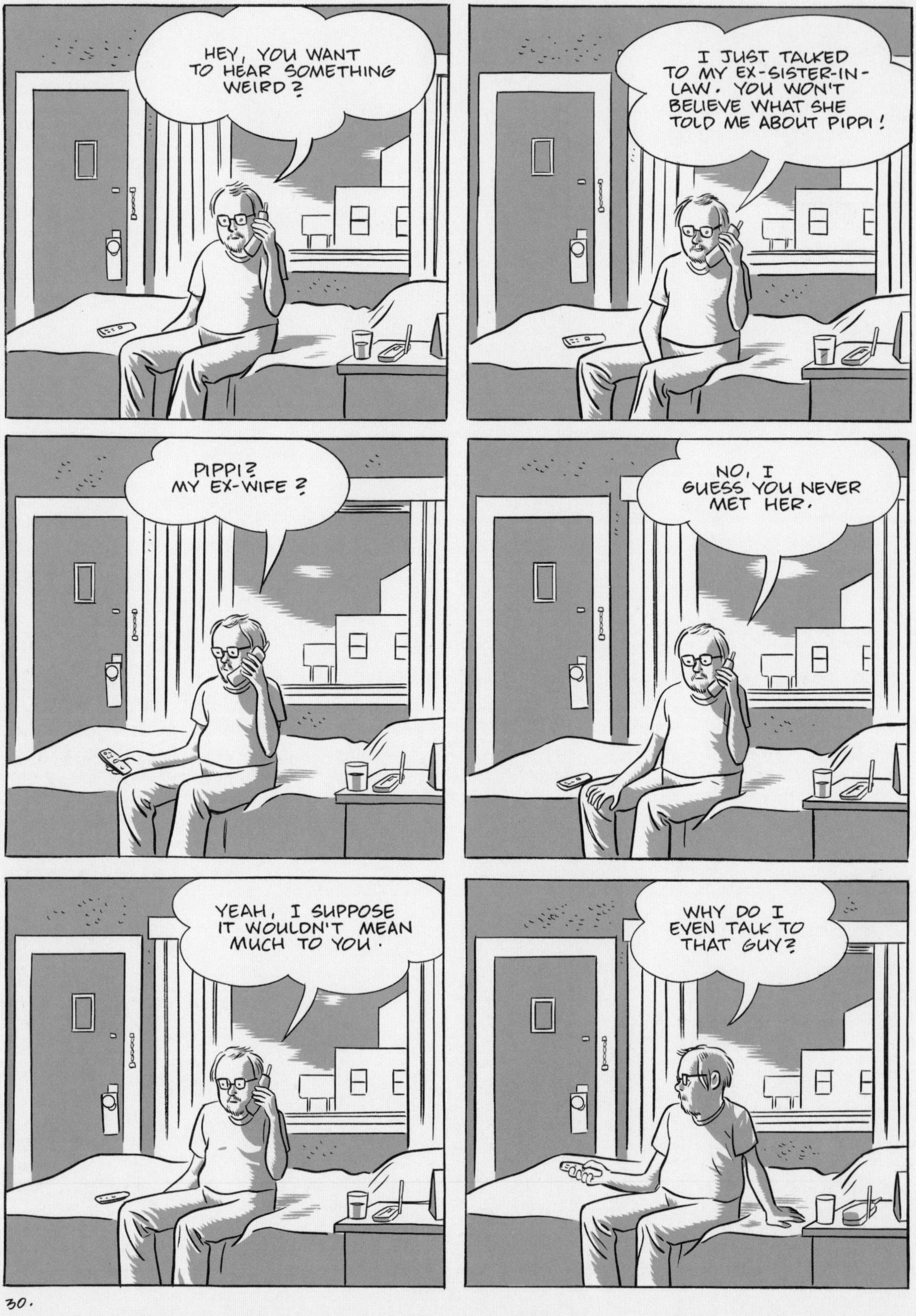
HEY, YOU WANT TO HEAR SOMETHING WEIRD?
I JUST TALKED TO MY EX-SISTER-IN-LAW. YOU WON'T BELIEVE WHAT SHE TOLD ME ABOUT PIPPI!
PIPPI? MY EX-WIFE?
NO, I GUESS YOU NEVER MET HER.
YEAH, I SUPPOSE IT WOULDN'T MEAN MUCH TO YOU.
WHY DO I EVEN TALK TO THAT GUY?

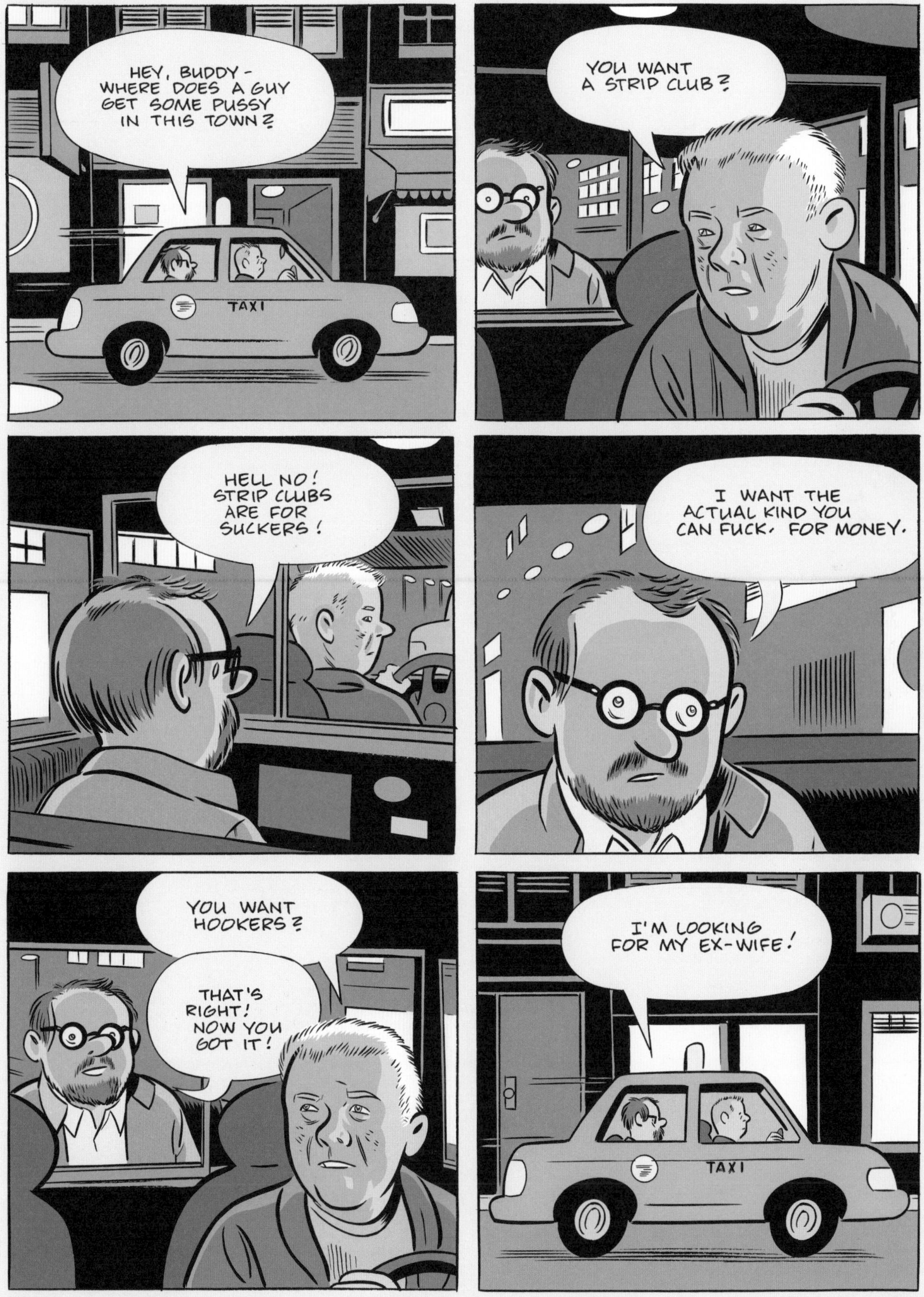
HEY, BUDDY - WHERE DOES A GUY GET SOME PUSSY IN THIS TOWN?
TAXI
YOU WANT A STRIP CLUB?
HELL NO! STRIP CLUBS ARE FOR SUCKERS!
I WANT THE ACTUAL KIND YOU CAN FUCK. FOR MONEY.
YOU WANT HOOKERS?
THAT'S RIGHT! NOW YOU GOT IT!
I'M LOOKING FOR MY EX-WIFE!
TAXI

THE DARK KNIGHT

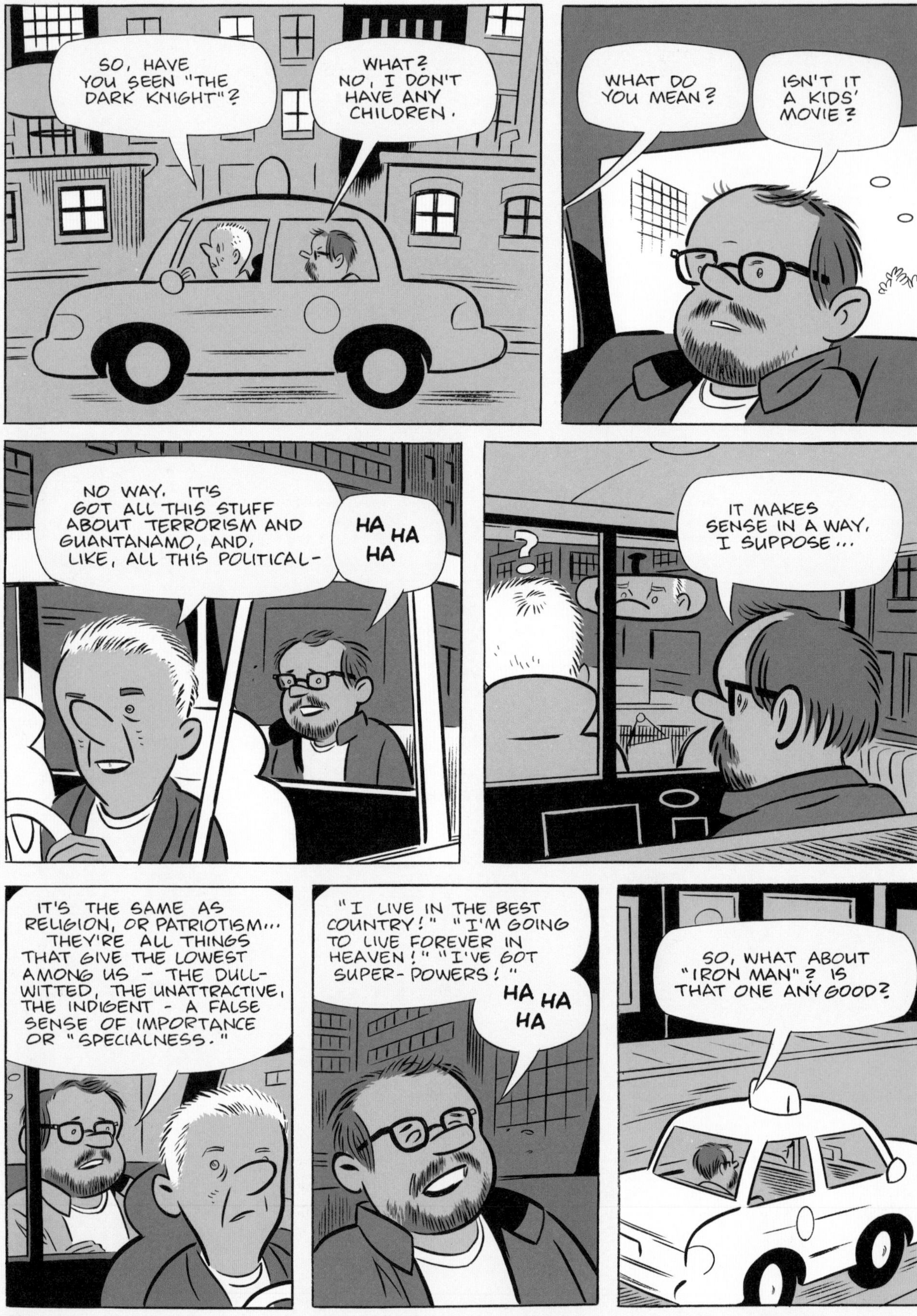

SO, HAVE YOU SEEN "THE DARK KNIGHT"?
WHAT? NO, I DON'T HAVE ANY CHILDREN.
WHAT DO YOU MEAN?
ISN'T IT A KIDS' MOVIE?
NO WAY. IT'S GOT ALL THIS STUFF ABOUT TERRORISM AND GUANTANAMO, AND, LIKE, ALL THIS POLITICAL-
HA HA HA
?
IT MAKES SENSE IN A WAY, I SUPPOSE...
IT'S THE SAME AS RELIGION, OR PATRIOTISM... THEY'RE ALL THINGS THAT GIVE THE LOWEST AMONG US - THE DULL-WITTED, THE UNATTRACTIVE, THE INDIGENT - A FALSE SENSE OF IMPORTANCE OR "SPECIALNESS."
"I LIVE IN THE BEST COUNTRY!" "I'M GOING TO LIVE FOREVER IN HEAVEN!" "I'VE GOT SUPER-POWERS!"
HA HA HA
SO, WHAT ABOUT "IRON MAN"? IS THAT ONE ANY GOOD?

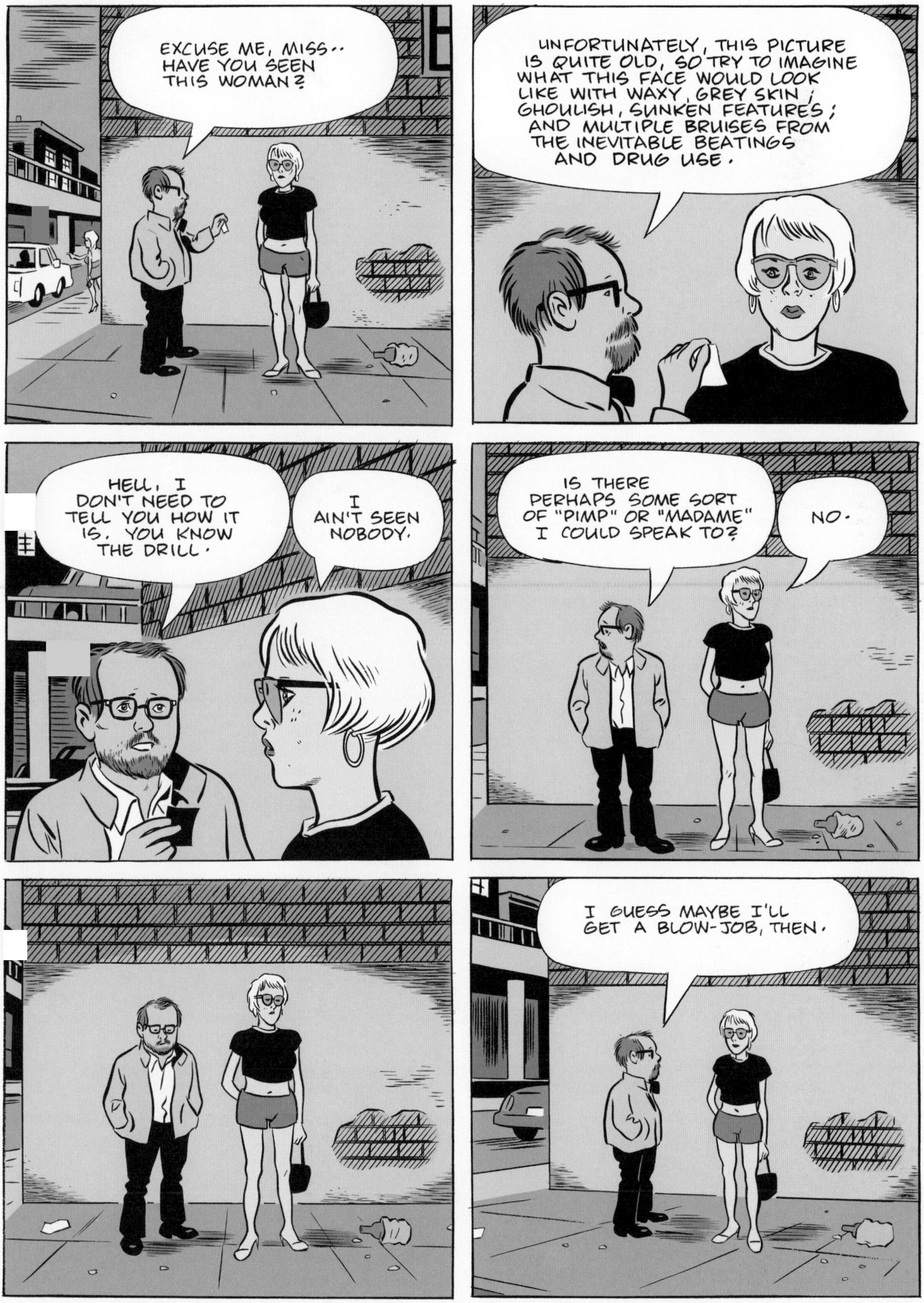
EXCUSE ME, MISS.. HAVE YOU SEEN THIS WOMAN?
UNFORTUNATELY, THIS PICTURE IS QUITE OLD, SO TRY TO IMAGINE WHAT THIS FACE WOULD LOOK LIKE WITH WAXY, GREY SKIN; GHOULISH, SUNKEN FEATURES; AND MULTIPLE BRUISES FROM THE INEVITABLE BEATINGS AND DRUG USE.
HELL, I DON'T NEED TO TELL YOU HOW IT IS. YOU KNOW THE DRILL.
I AIN'T SEEN NOBODY.
IS THERE PERHAPS SOME SORT OF "PIMP" OR "MADAME" I COULD SPEAK TO?
NO.
I GUESS MAYBE I'LL GET A BLOW-JOB, THEN.

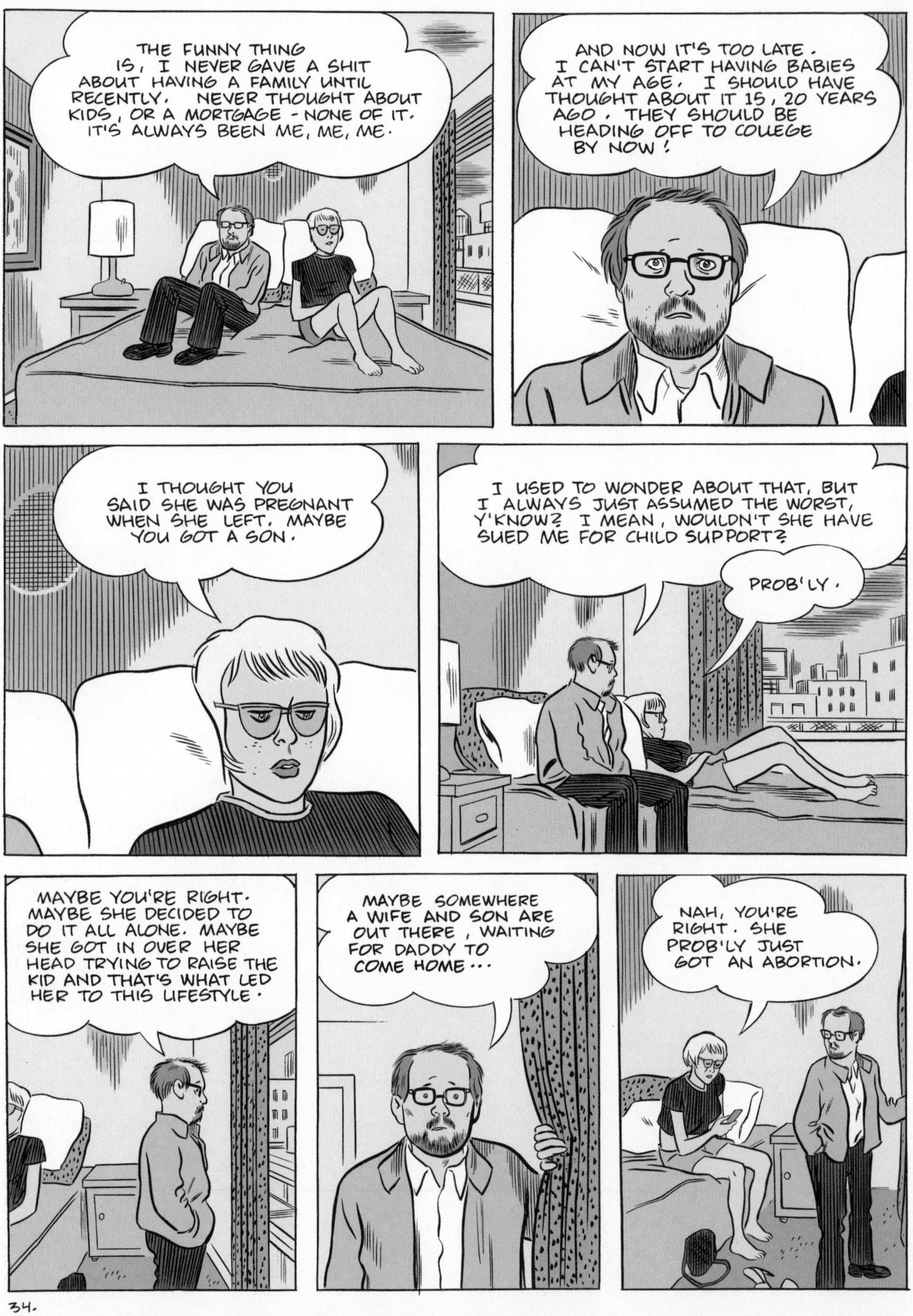
THE FUNNY THING IS, I NEVER GAVE A SHIT ABOUT HAVING A FAMILY UNTIL RECENTLY. NEVER THOUGHT ABOUT KIDS, OR A MORTGAGE - NONE OF IT. IT'S ALWAYS BEEN ME, ME, ME.
AND NOW IT'S TOO LATE. I CAN'T START HAVING BABIES AT MY AGE. I SHOULD HAVE THOUGHT ABOUT IT 15, 20 YEARS AGO. THEY SHOULD BE HEADING OFF TO COLLEGE BY NOW!
I THOUGHT YOU SAID SHE WAS PREGNANT WHEN SHE LEFT. MAYBE YOU GOT A SON.
I USED TO WONDER ABOUT THAT, BUT I ALWAYS JUST ASSUMED THE WORST, Y'KNOW? I MEAN, WOULDN'T SHE HAVE SUED ME FOR CHILD SUPPORT?
PROB'LY.
MAYBE YOU'RE RIGHT. MAYBE SHE DECIDED TO DO IT ALL ALONE. MAYBE SHE GOT IN OVER HER HEAD TRYING TO RAISE THE KID AND THAT'S WHAT LED HER TO THIS LIFESTYLE.
MAYBE SOMEWHERE A WIFE AND SON ARE OUT THERE, WAITING FOR DADDY TO COME HOME...
NAH, YOU'RE RIGHT. SHE PROB'LY JUST GOT AN ABORTION.

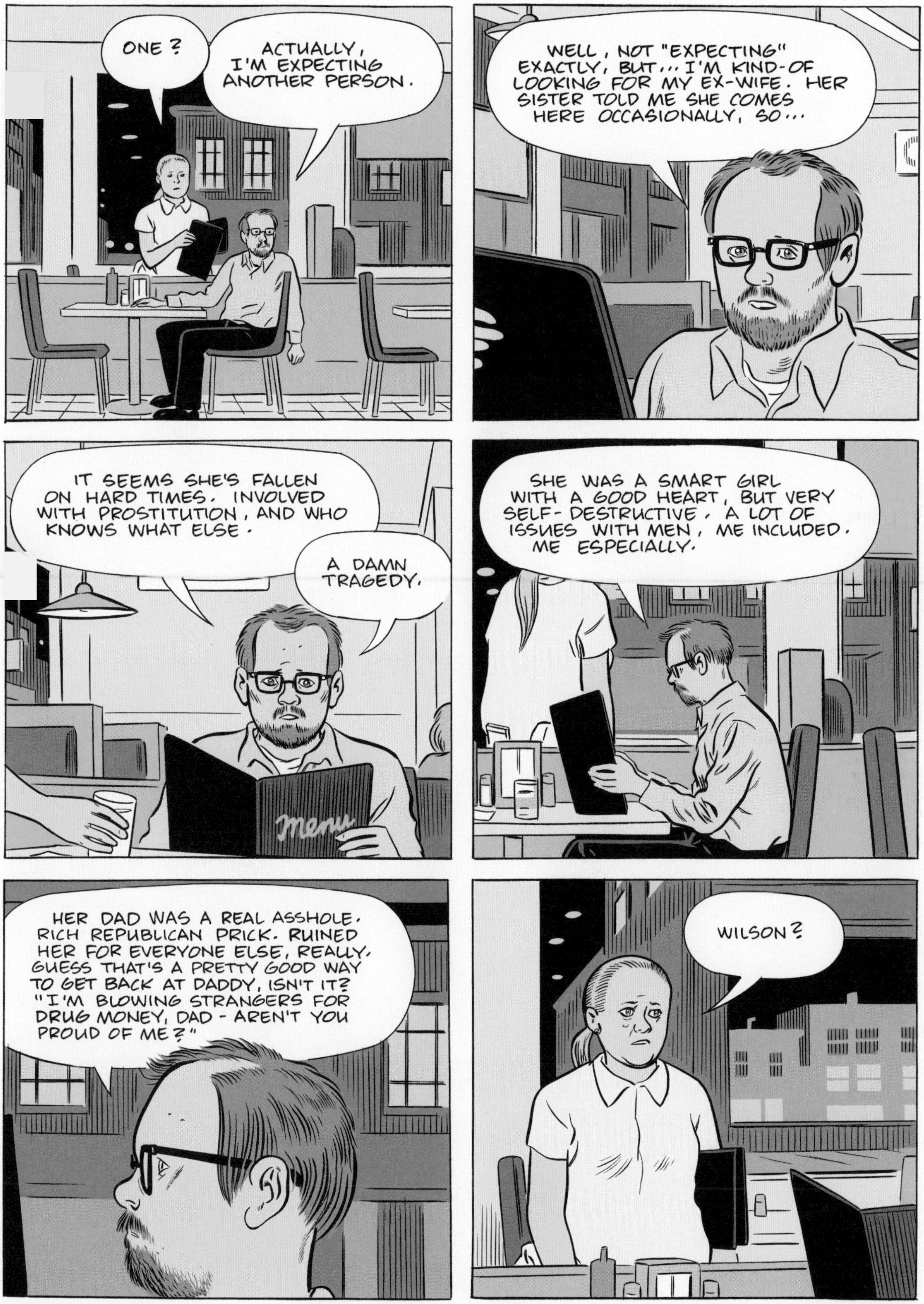
ONE ?
ACTUALLY, I'M EXPECTING ANOTHER PERSON.
WELL, NOT "EXPECTING" EXACTLY, BUT... I'M KIND-OF LOOKING FOR MY EX-WIFE. HER SISTER TOLD ME SHE COMES HERE OCCASIONALLY, SO...
IT SEEMS SHE'S FALLEN ON HARD TIMES. INVOLVED WITH PROSTITUTION, AND WHO KNOWS WHAT ELSE.
A DAMN TRAGEDY.
Menu
SHE WAS A SMART GIRL WITH A GOOD HEART, BUT VERY SELF-DESTRUCTIVE. A LOT OF ISSUES WITH MEN, ME INCLUDED. ME ESPECIALLY.
HER DAD WAS A REAL ASSHOLE. RICH REPUBLICAN PRICK. RUINED HER FOR EVERYONE ELSE, REALLY. GUESS THAT'S A PRETTY GOOD WAY TO GET BACK AT DADDY, ISN'T IT? "I'M BLOWING STRANGERS FOR DRUG MONEY, DAD - AREN'T YOU PROUD OF ME?"
WILSON?

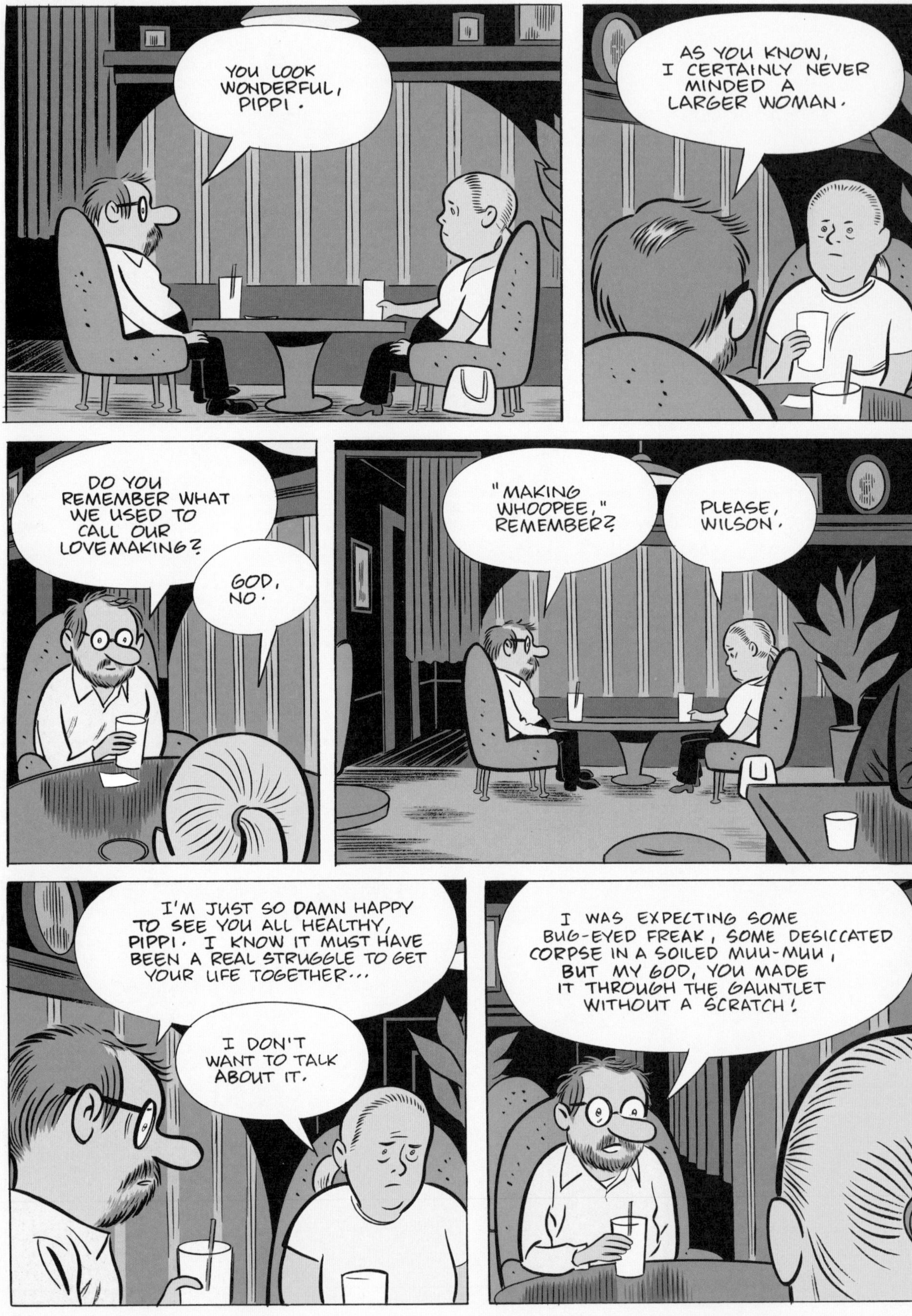

YOU LOOK WONDERFUL, PIPPI.
AS YOU KNOW, I CERTAINLY NEVER MINDED A LARGER WOMAN.
DO YOU REMEMBER WHAT WE USED TO CALL OUR LOVEMAKING?
GOD, NO.
"MAKING WHOOPEE," REMEMBER?
PLEASE, WILSON.
I'M JUST SO DAMN HAPPY TO SEE YOU ALL HEALTHY, PIPPI. I KNOW IT MUST HAVE BEEN A REAL STRUGGLE TO GET YOUR LIFE TOGETHER...
I DON'T WANT TO TALK ABOUT IT.
I WAS EXPECTING SOME BUG-EYED FREAK, SOME DESICCATED CORPSE IN A SOILED MUU-MUU, BUT MY GOD, YOU MADE IT THROUGH THE GAUNTLET WITHOUT A SCRATCH!

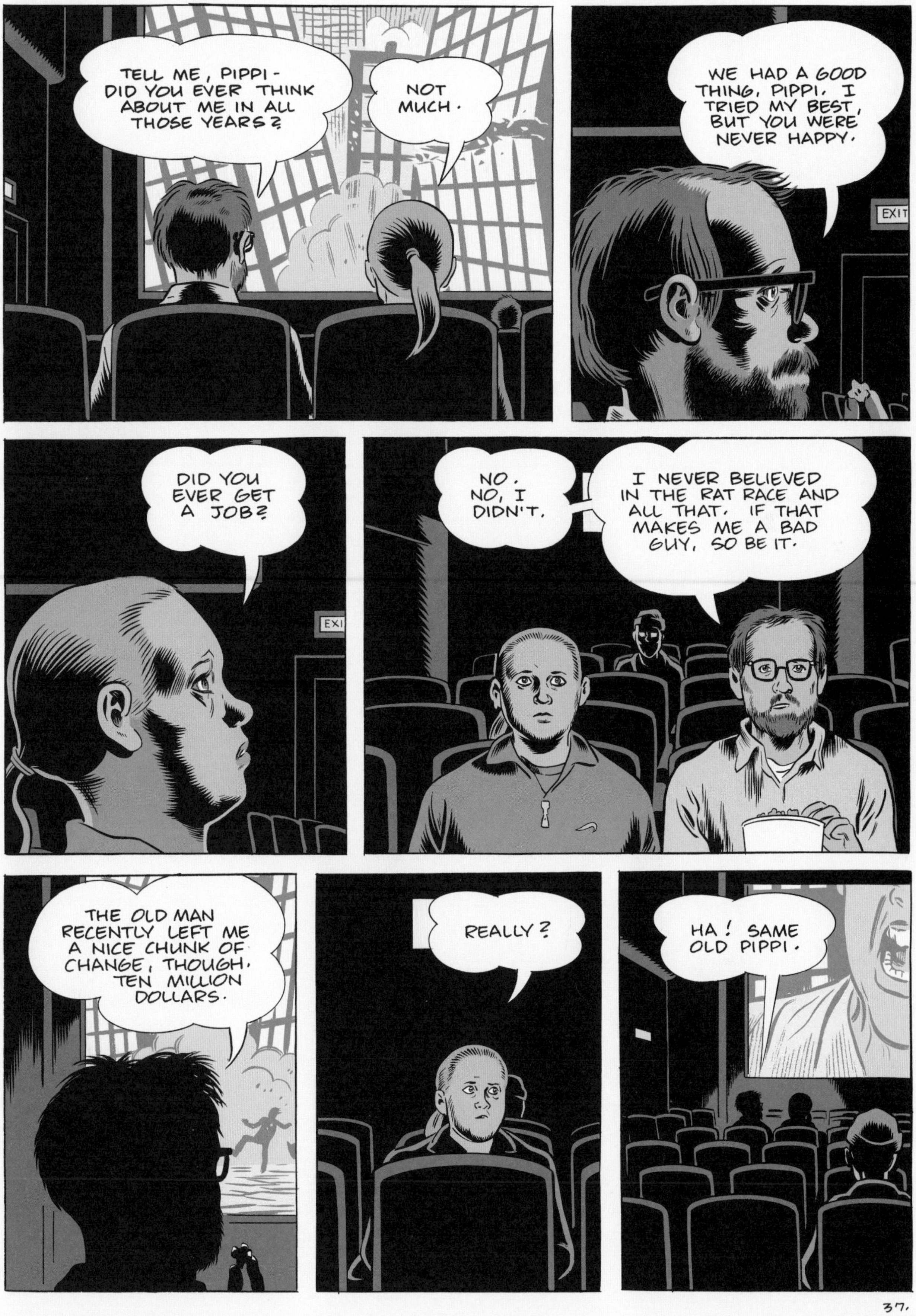
TELL ME, PIPPI - DID YOU EVER THINK ABOUT ME IN ALL THOSE YEARS?
NOT MUCH.
WE HAD A GOOD THING, PIPPI. I TRIED MY BEST, BUT YOU WERE NEVER HAPPY.
EXIT
DID YOU EVER GET A JOB?
EXI
NO. NO, I DIDN'T.
I NEVER BELIEVED IN THE RAT RACE AND ALL THAT. IF THAT MAKES ME A BAD GUY, SO BE IT.
THE OLD MAN RECENTLY LEFT ME A NICE CHUNK OF CHANGE, THOUGH. TEN MILLION DOLLARS.
REALLY?
HA! SAME OLD PIPPI.

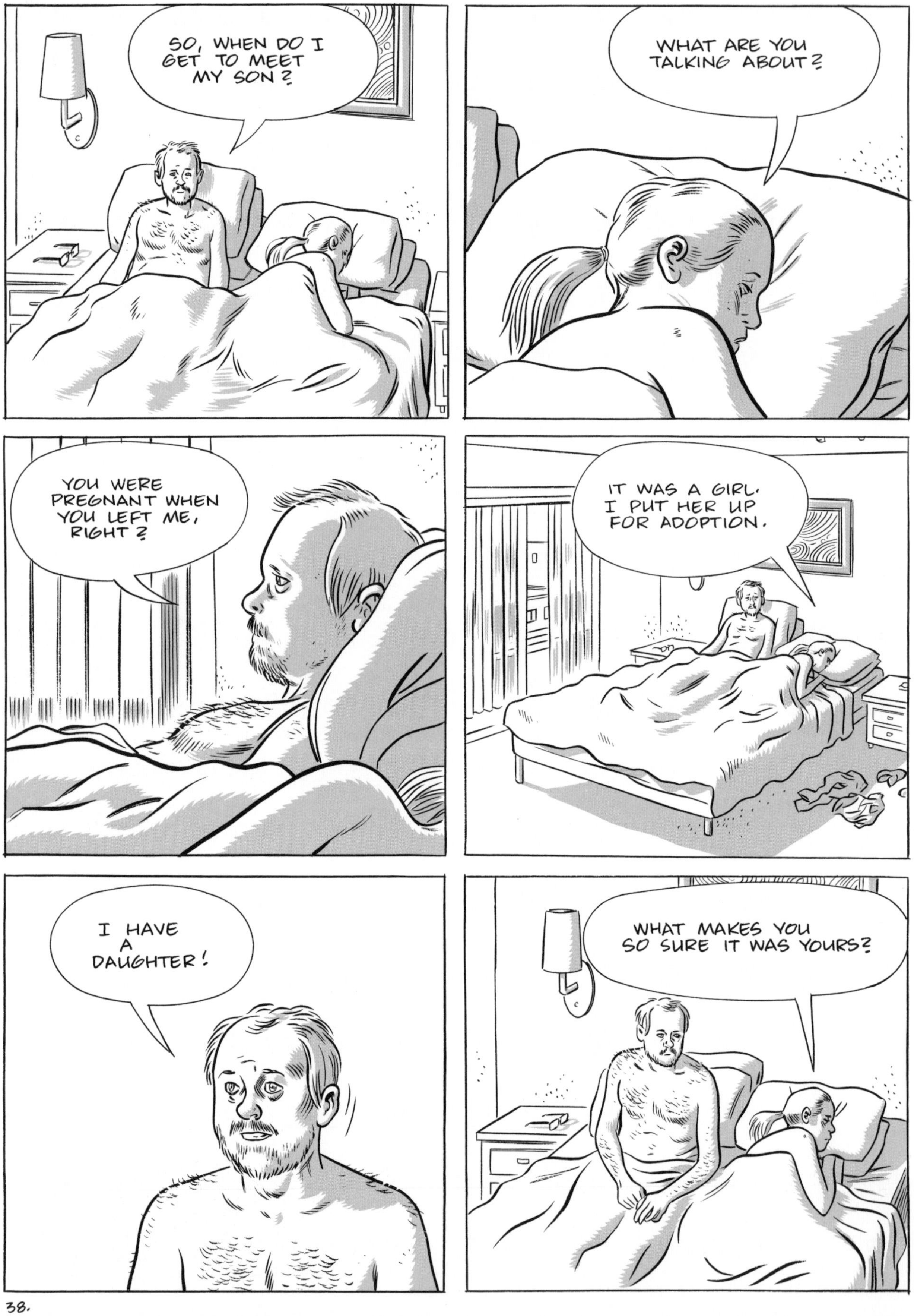
SO, WHEN DO I GET TO MEET MY SON?
WHAT ARE YOU TALKING ABOUT?
YOU WERE PREGNANT WHEN YOU LEFT ME, RIGHT?
IT WAS A GIRL. I PUT HER UP FOR ADOPTION.
I HAVE A DAUGHTER!
WHAT MAKES YOU SO SURE IT WAS YOURS?

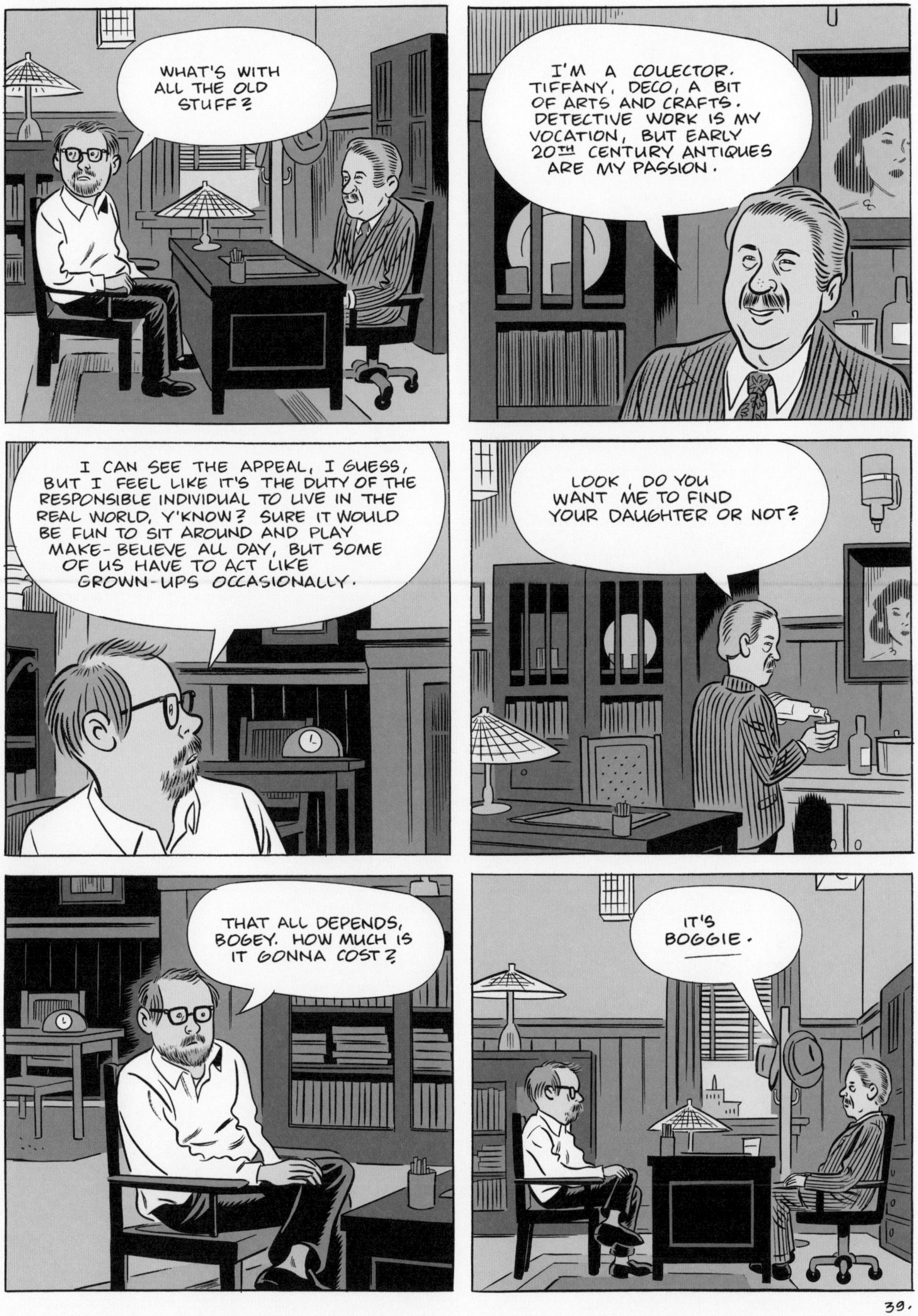
WHAT'S WITH ALL THE OLD STUFF?
I'M A COLLECTOR. TIFFANY, DECO, A BIT OF ARTS AND CRAFTS. DETECTIVE WORK IS MY VOCATION, BUT EARLY 20TH CENTURY ANTIQUES ARE MY PASSION.
I CAN SEE THE APPEAL, I GUESS, BUT I FEEL LIKE IT'S THE DUTY OF THE RESPONSIBLE INDIVIDUAL TO LIVE IN THE REAL WORLD, Y'KNOW? SURE IT WOULD BE FUN TO SIT AROUND AND PLAY MAKE-BELIEVE ALL DAY, BUT SOME OF US HAVE TO ACT LIKE GROWN-UPS OCCASIONALLY.
LOOK, DO YOU WANT ME TO FIND YOUR DAUGHTER OR NOT?
THAT ALL DEPENDS, BOGEY. HOW MUCH IS IT GONNA COST?
IT'S BOGGIE.

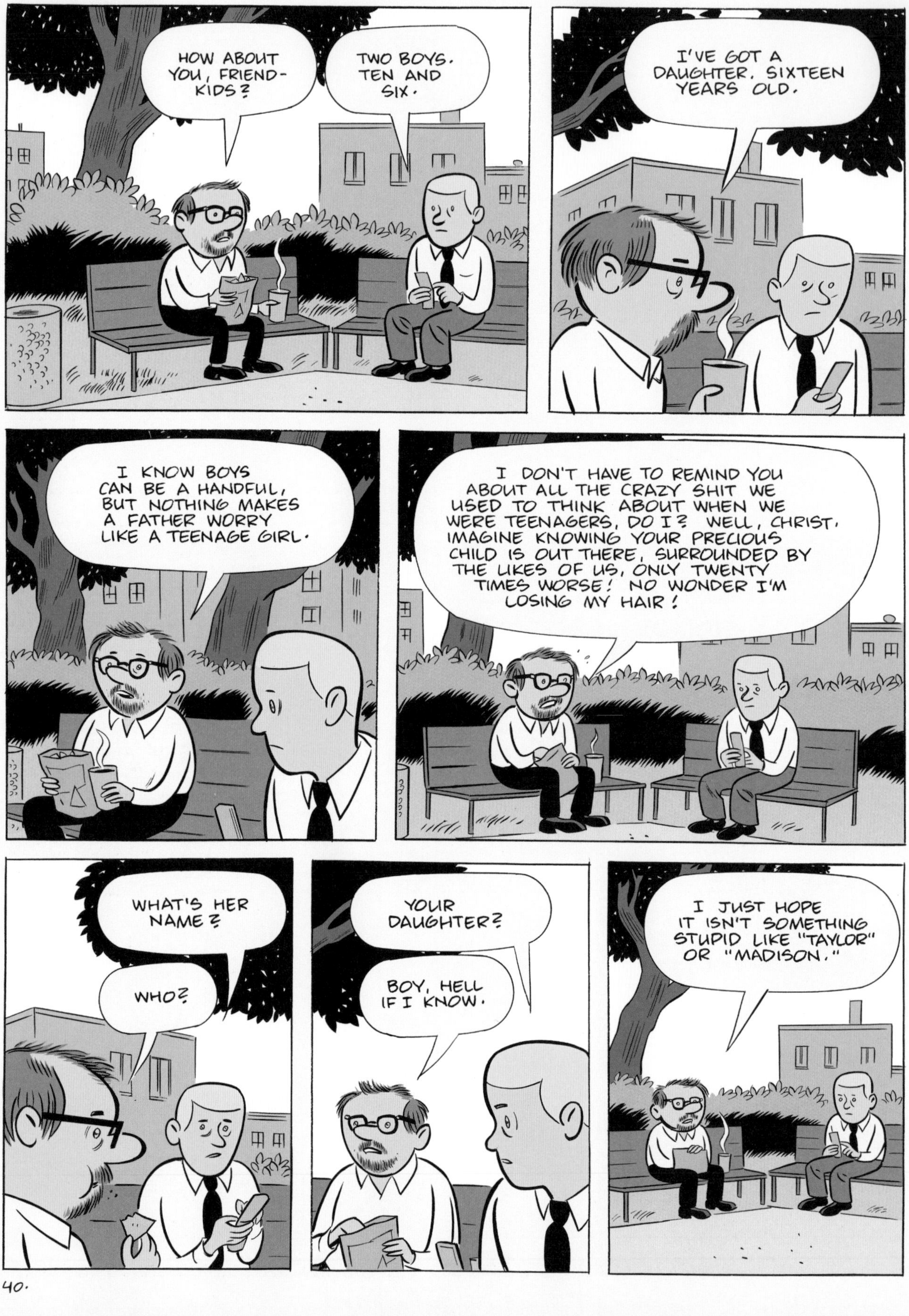
HOW ABOUT YOU, FRIEND- KIDS?
TWO BOYS. TEN AND SIX.
I'VE GOT A DAUGHTER. SIXTEEN YEARS OLD.
I KNOW BOYS CAN BE A HANDFUL, BUT NOTHING MAKES A FATHER WORRY LIKE A TEENAGE GIRL.
I DON'T HAVE TO REMIND YOU ABOUT ALL THE CRAZY SHIT WE USED TO THINK ABOUT WHEN WE WERE TEENAGERS, DO I? WELL, CHRIST. IMAGINE KNOWING YOUR PRECIOUS CHILD IS OUT THERE, SURROUNDED BY THE LIKES OF US, ONLY TWENTY TIMES WORSE! NO WONDER I'M LOSING MY HAIR!
WHAT'S HER NAME?
WHO?
YOUR DAUGHTER?
BOY, HELL IF I KNOW.
I JUST HOPE IT ISN'T SOMETHING STUPID LIKE "TAYLOR" OR "MADISON."

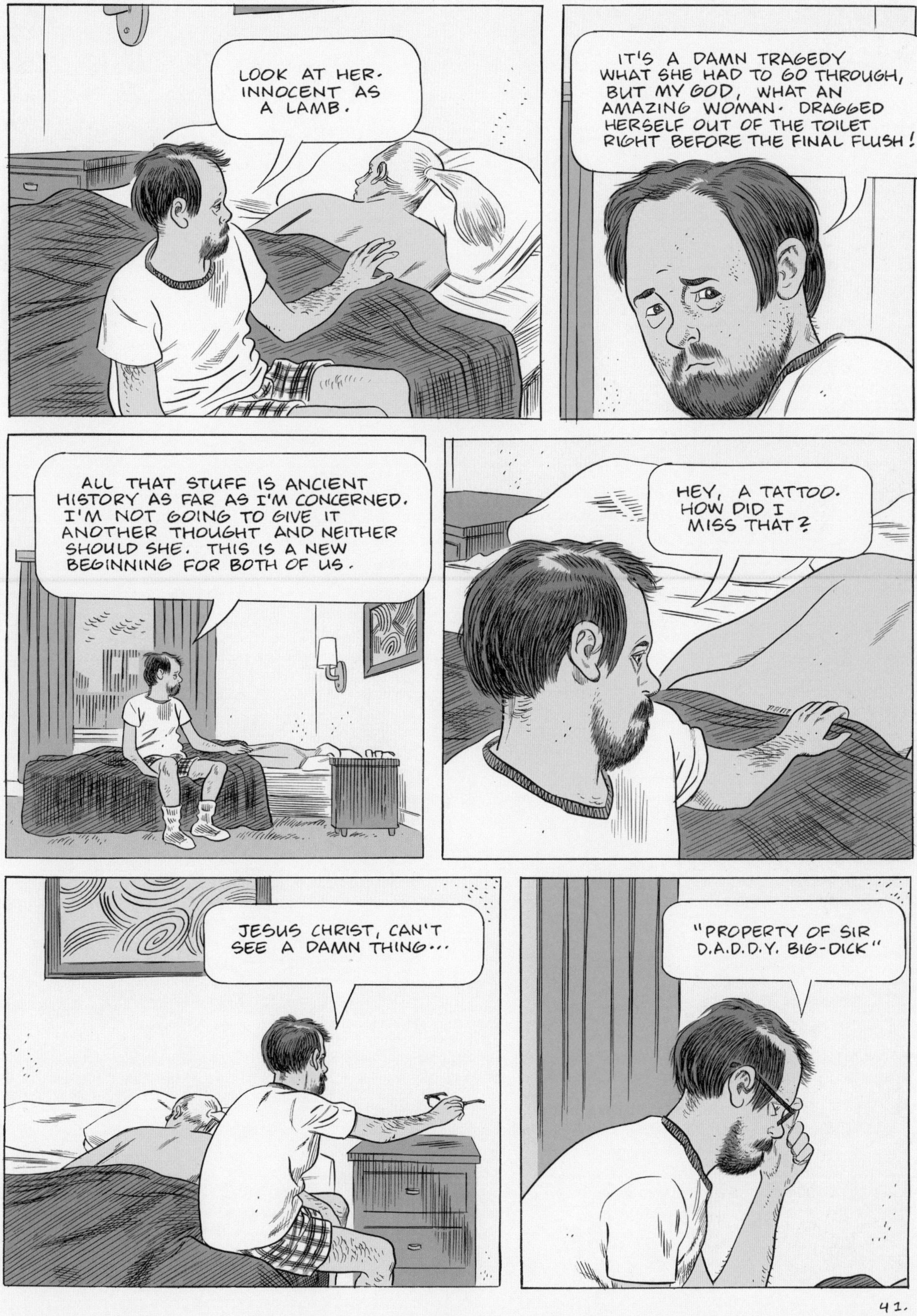
LOOK AT HER. INNOCENT AS A LAMB.
IT'S A DAMN TRAGEDY WHAT SHE HAD TO GO THROUGH, BUT MY GOD, WHAT AN AMAZING WOMAN. DRAGGED HERSELF OUT OF THE TOILET RIGHT BEFORE THE FINAL FLUSH!
ALL THAT STUFF IS ANCIENT HISTORY AS FAR AS I'M CONCERNED. I'M NOT GOING TO GIVE IT ANOTHER THOUGHT AND NEITHER SHOULD SHE. THIS IS A NEW BEGINNING FOR BOTH OF US.
HEY, A TATTOO. HOW DID I MISS THAT?
JESUS CHRIST, CAN'T SEE A DAMN THING...
"PROPERTY OF SIR D.A.D.D.Y. BIG-DICK"

STAKEOUT

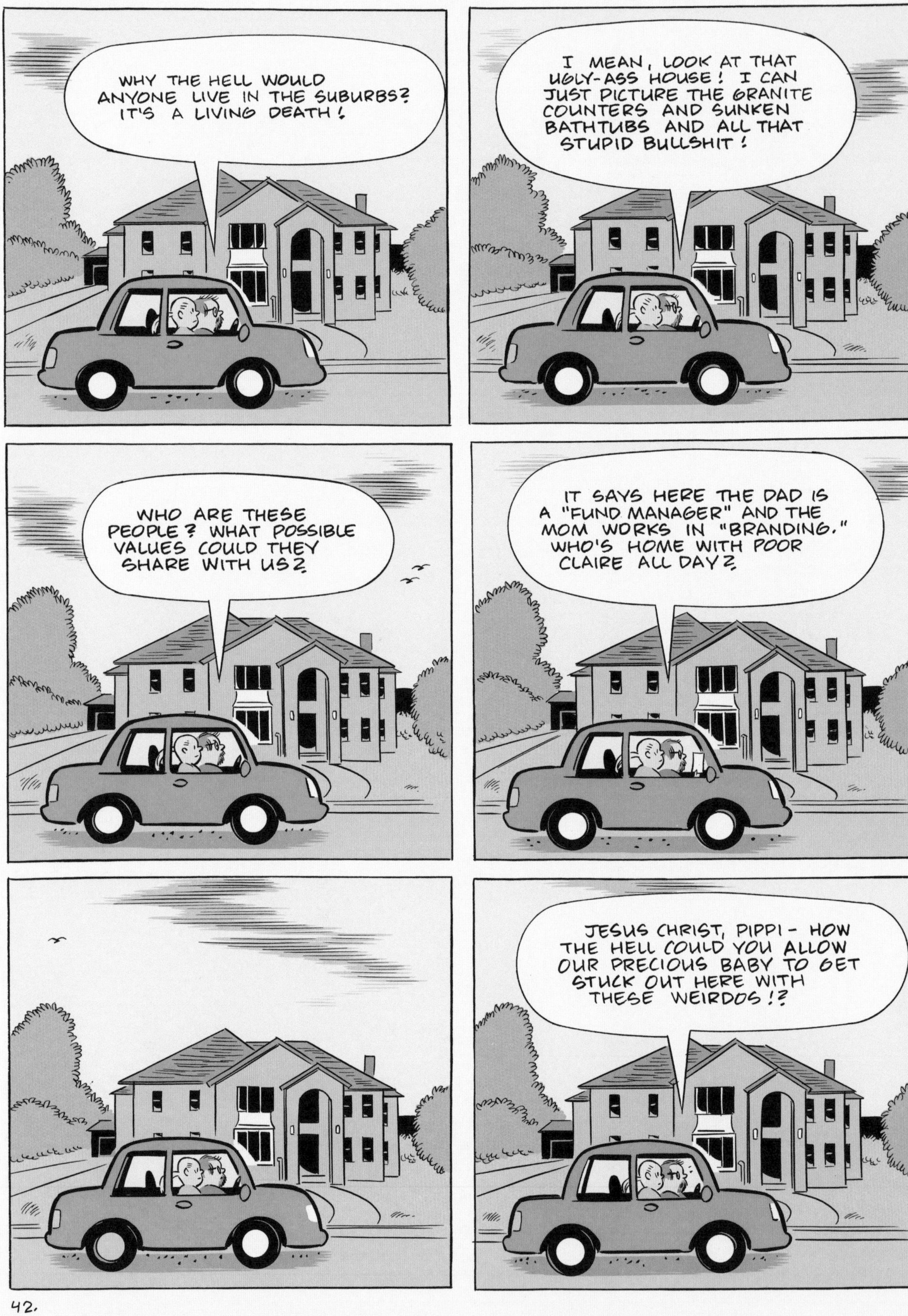
WHY THE HELL WOULD ANYONE LIVE IN THE SUBURBS? IT'S A LIVING DEATH!
I MEAN, LOOK AT THAT UGLY-ASS HOUSE! I CAN JUST PICTURE THE GRANITE COUNTERS AND SUNKEN BATHTUBS AND ALL THAT STUPID BULLSHIT!
WHO ARE THESE PEOPLE? WHAT POSSIBLE VALUES COULD THEY SHARE WITH US?
IT SAYS HERE THE DAD IS A "FUND MANAGER" AND THE MOM WORKS IN "BRANDING." WHO'S HOME WITH POOR CLAIRE ALL DAY?
JESUS CHRIST, PIPPI - HOW THE HELL COULD YOU ALLOW OUR PRECIOUS BABY TO GET STUCK OUT HERE WITH THESE WEIRDOS!?

SHOPPING MALL

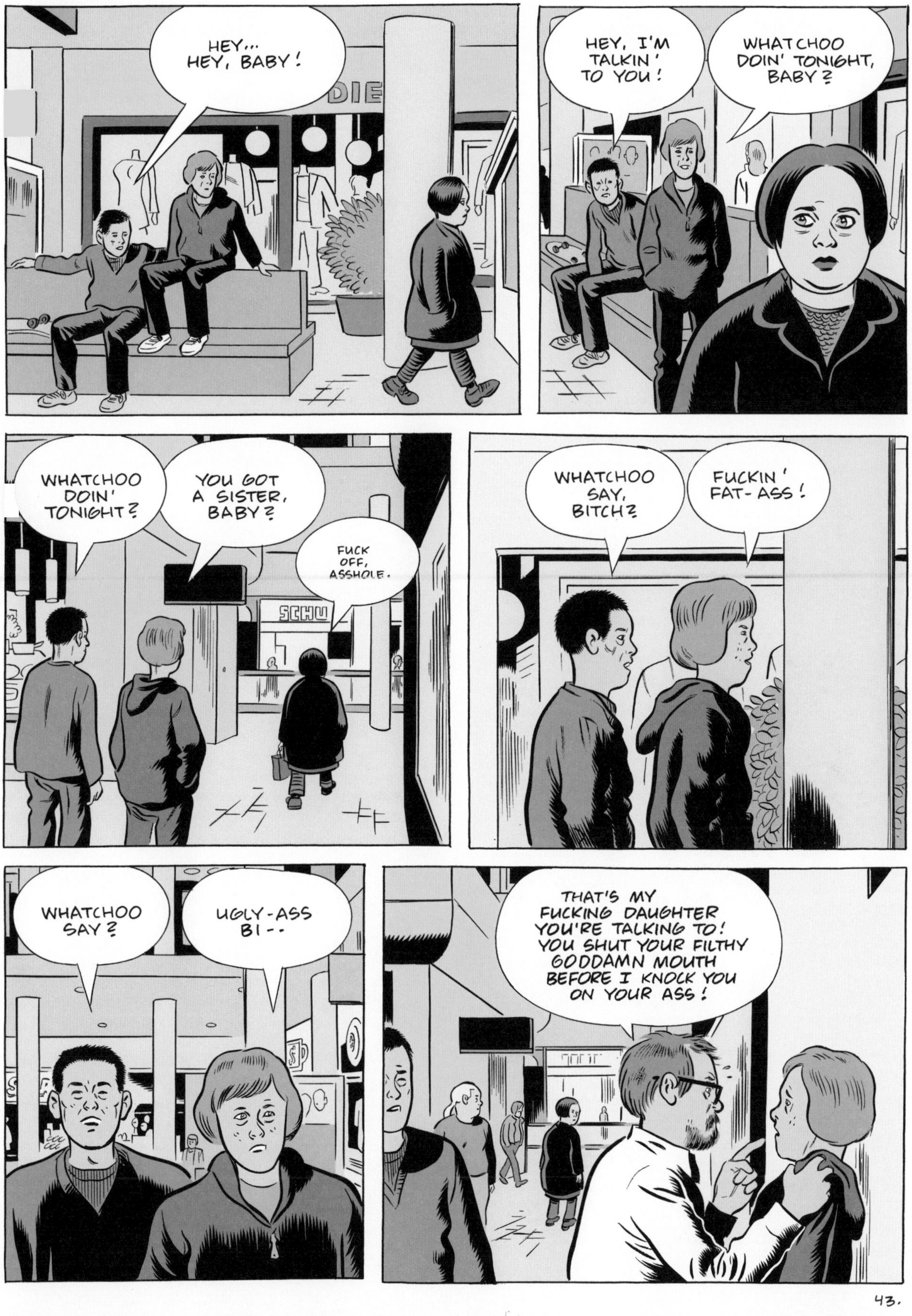
HEY... HEY, BABY!
DIE
HEY, I'M TALKIN' TO YOU!
WHATCHOO DOIN' TONIGHT, BABY?
WHATCHOO DOIN' TONIGHT?
YOU GOT A SISTER, BABY?
FUCK OFF, ASSHOLE.
SCHU
WHATCHOO SAY, BITCH?
FUCKIN' FAT-ASS!
WHATCHOO SAY?
UGLY-ASS BI--
THAT'S MY FUCKING DAUGHTER YOU'RE TALKING TO! YOU SHUT YOUR FILTHY GODDAMN MOUTH BEFORE I KNOCK YOU ON YOUR ASS!

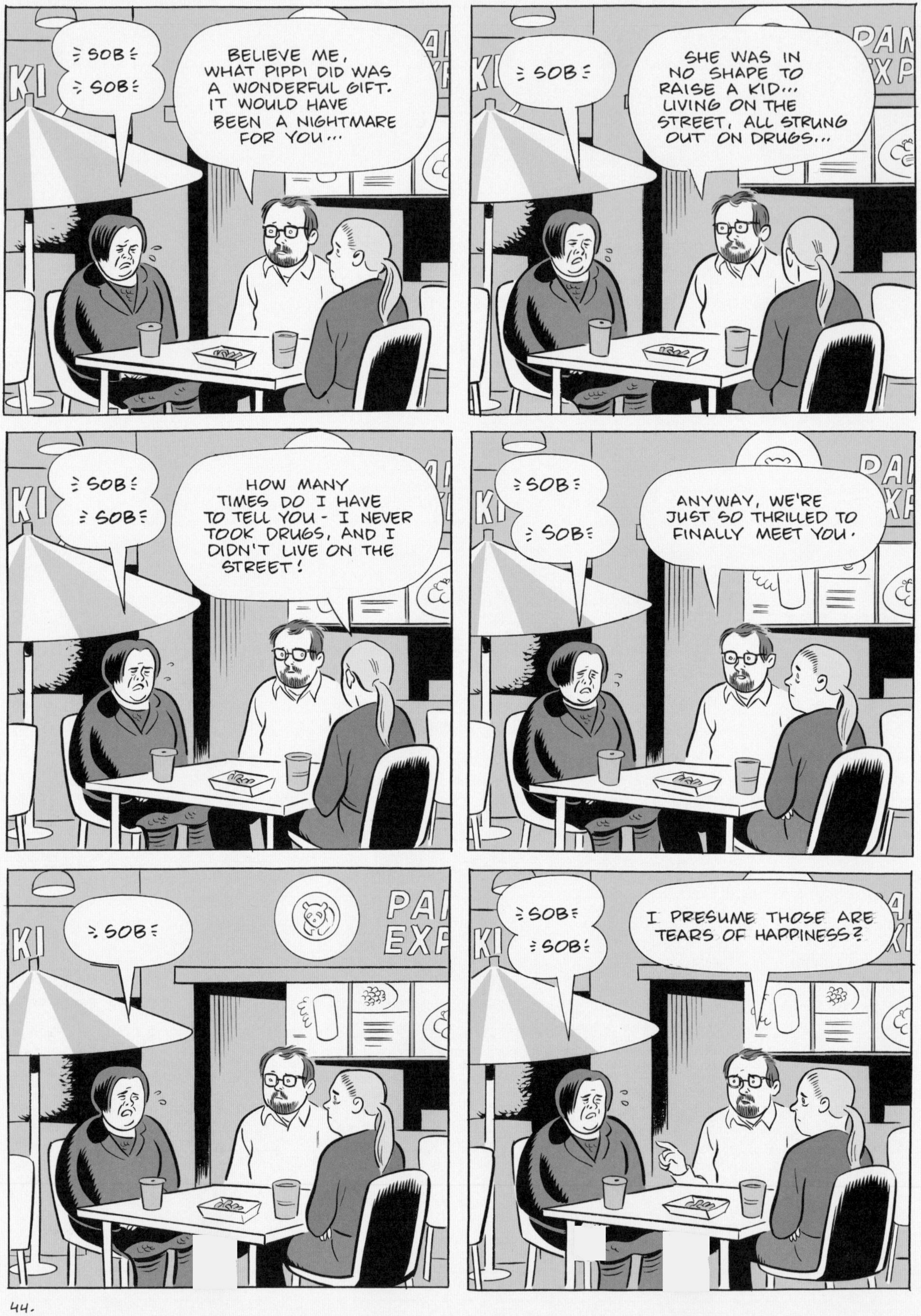
SOB
SOB
BELIEVE ME, WHAT PIPPI DID WAS A WONDERFUL GIFT. IT WOULD HAVE BEEN A NIGHTMARE FOR YOU...
SOB
SHE WAS IN NO SHAPE TO RAISE A KID... LIVING ON THE STREET, ALL STRUNG OUT ON DRUGS...
SOB
SOB
HOW MANY TIMES DO I HAVE TO TELL YOU - I NEVER TOOK DRUGS, AND I DIDN'T LIVE ON THE STREET!
SOB
SOB
ANYWAY, WE'RE JUST SO THRILLED TO FINALLY MEET YOU.
SOB
SOB
SOB
I PRESUME THOSE ARE TEARS OF HAPPINESS?

NATURE WALK

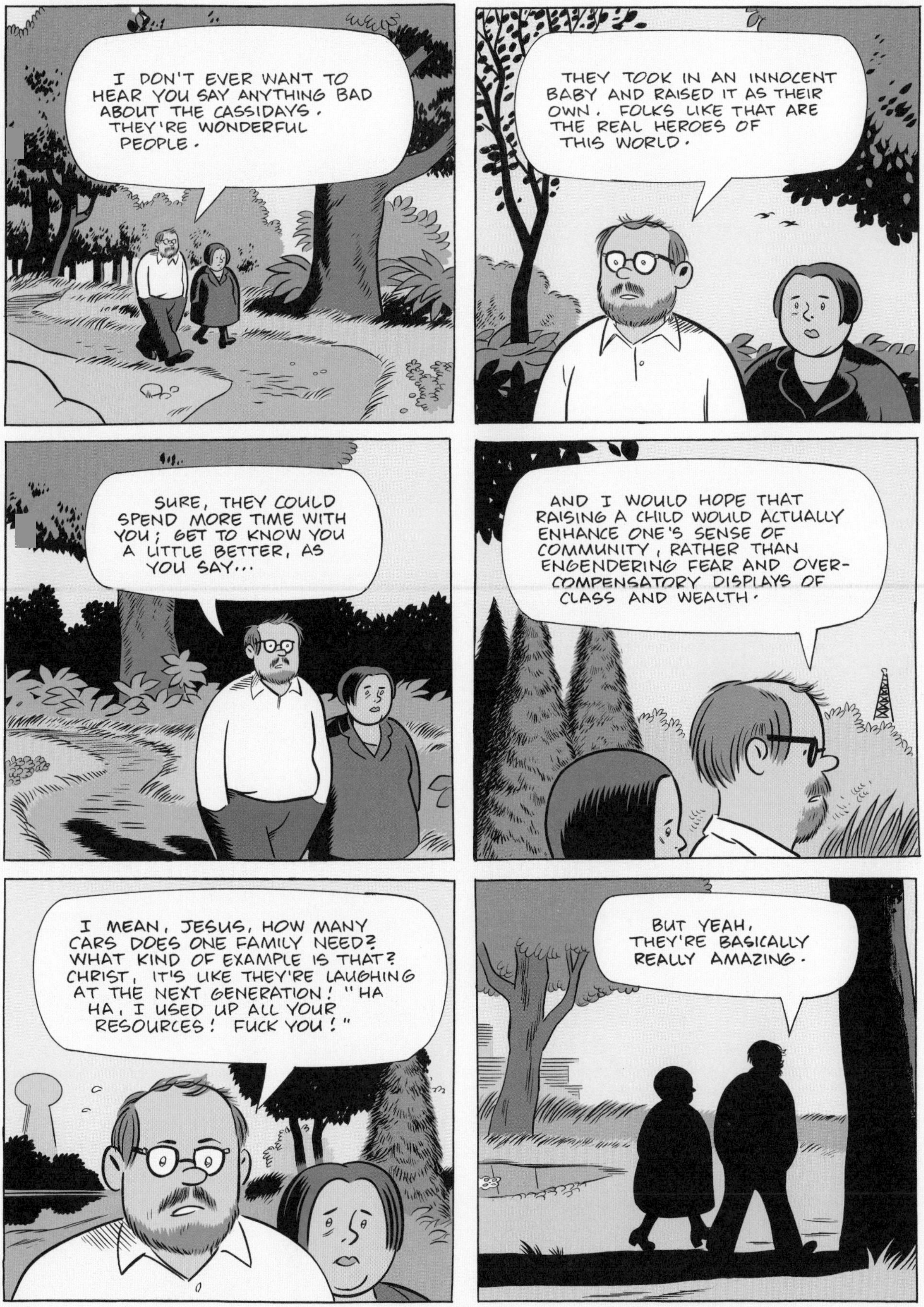
I DON'T EVER WANT TO HEAR YOU SAY ANYTHING BAD ABOUT THE CASSIDAYS. THEY'RE WONDERFUL PEOPLE.
THEY TOOK IN AN INNOCENT BABY AND RAISED IT AS THEIR OWN. FOLKS LIKE THAT ARE THE REAL HEROES OF THIS WORLD.
SURE, THEY COULD SPEND MORE TIME WITH YOU; GET TO KNOW YOU A LITTLE BETTER, AS YOU SAY...
AND I WOULD HOPE THAT RAISING A CHILD WOULD ACTUALLY ENHANCE ONE'S SENSE OF COMMUNITY, RATHER THAN ENGENDERING FEAR AND OVER-COMPENSATORY DISPLAYS OF CLASS AND WEALTH.
I MEAN, JESUS, HOW MANY CARS DOES ONE FAMILY NEED? WHAT KIND OF EXAMPLE IS THAT? CHRIST, IT'S LIKE THEY'RE LAUGHING AT THE NEXT GENERATION! "HA HA, I USED UP ALL YOUR RESOURCES! FUCK YOU!"
BUT YEAH, THEY'RE BASICALLY REALLY AMAZING.

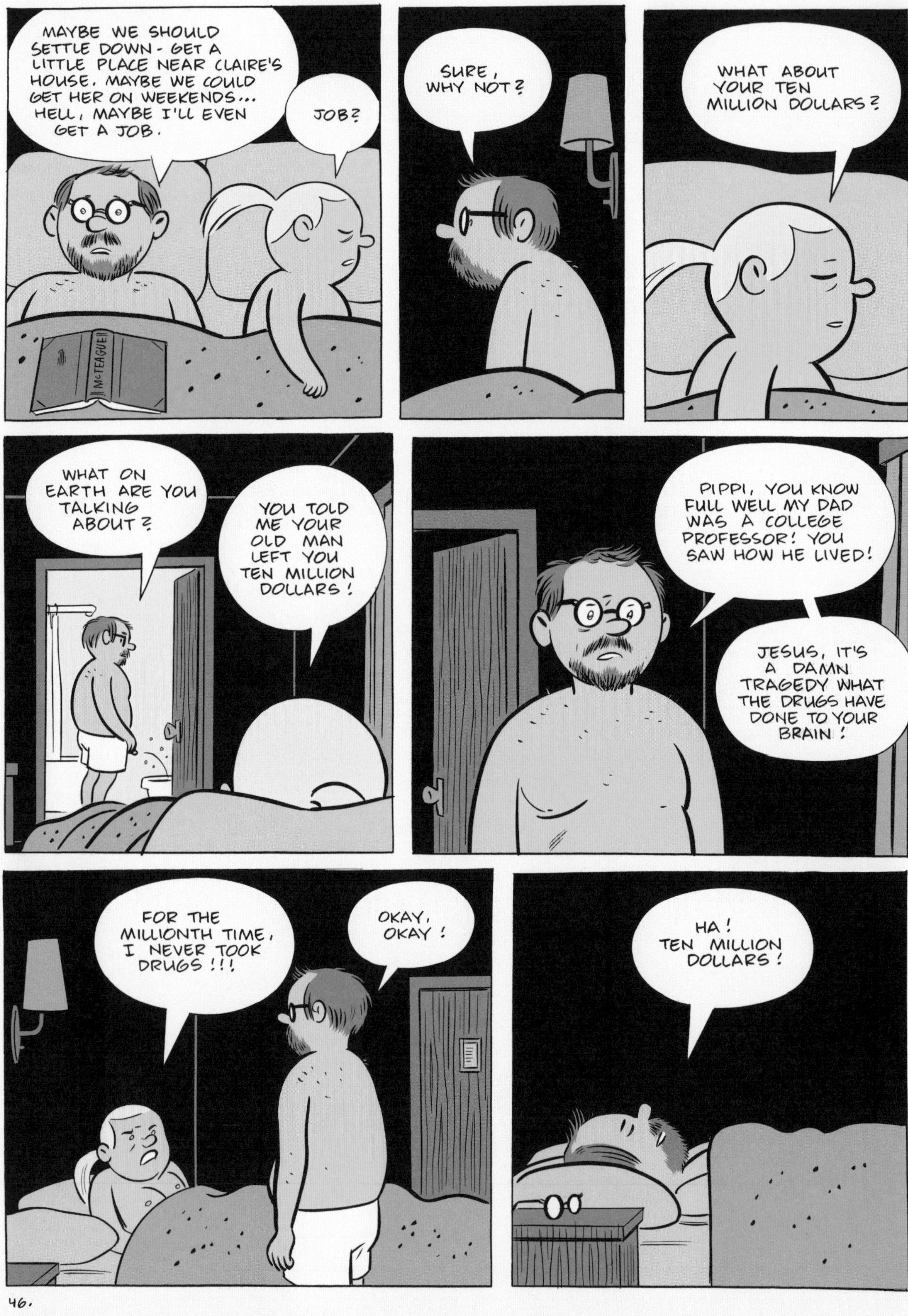
MAYBE WE SHOULD SETTLE DOWN - GET A LITTLE PLACE NEAR CLAIRE'S HOUSE. MAYBE WE COULD GET HER ON WEEKENDS... HELL, MAYBE I'LL EVEN GET A JOB.
JOB?
McTEAGUE
SURE, WHY NOT?
WHAT ABOUT YOUR TEN MILLION DOLLARS?
WHAT ON EARTH ARE YOU TALKING ABOUT?
YOU TOLD ME YOUR OLD MAN LEFT YOU TEN MILLION DOLLARS!
PIPPI, YOU KNOW FULL WELL MY DAD WAS A COLLEGE PROFESSOR! YOU SAW HOW HE LIVED!
JESUS, IT'S A DAMN TRAGEDY WHAT THE DRUGS HAVE DONE TO YOUR BRAIN!
FOR THE MILLIONTH TIME, I NEVER TOOK DRUGS!!!
OKAY, OKAY!
HA! TEN MILLION DOLLARS!

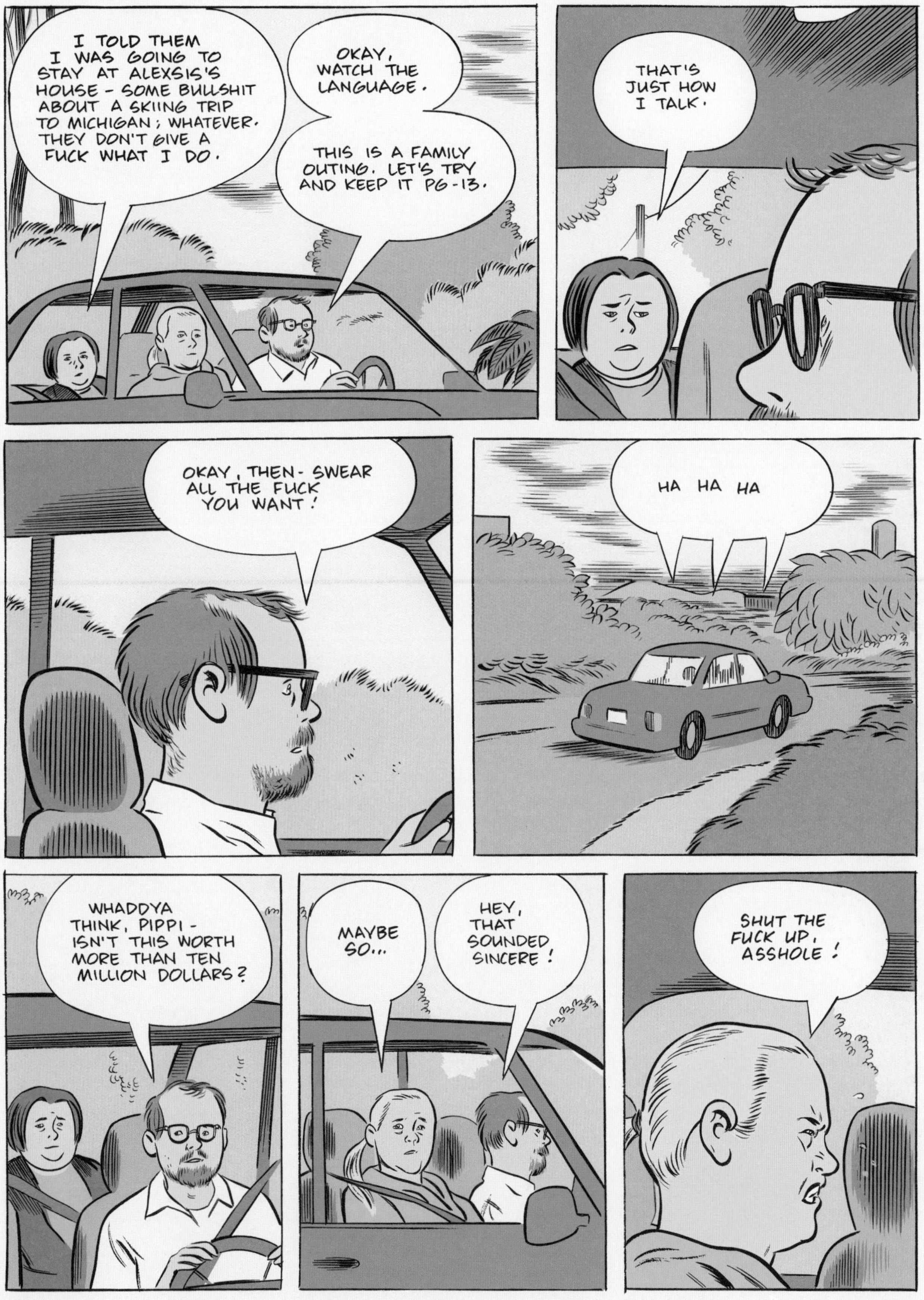
I TOLD THEM I WAS GOING TO STAY AT ALEXSIS'S HOUSE - SOME BULLSHIT ABOUT A SKIING TRIP TO MICHIGAN; WHATEVER. THEY DON'T GIVE A FUCK WHAT I DO.
OKAY, WATCH THE LANGUAGE.
THIS IS A FAMILY OUTING. LET'S TRY AND KEEP IT PG-13.
THAT'S JUST HOW I TALK.
OKAY, THEN- SWEAR ALL THE FUCK YOU WANT!
HA HA HA
WHADDYA THINK, PIPPI - ISN'T THIS WORTH MORE THAN TEN MILLION DOLLARS?
MAYBE SO...
HEY, THAT SOUNDED SINCERE!
SHUT THE FUCK UP, ASSHOLE!

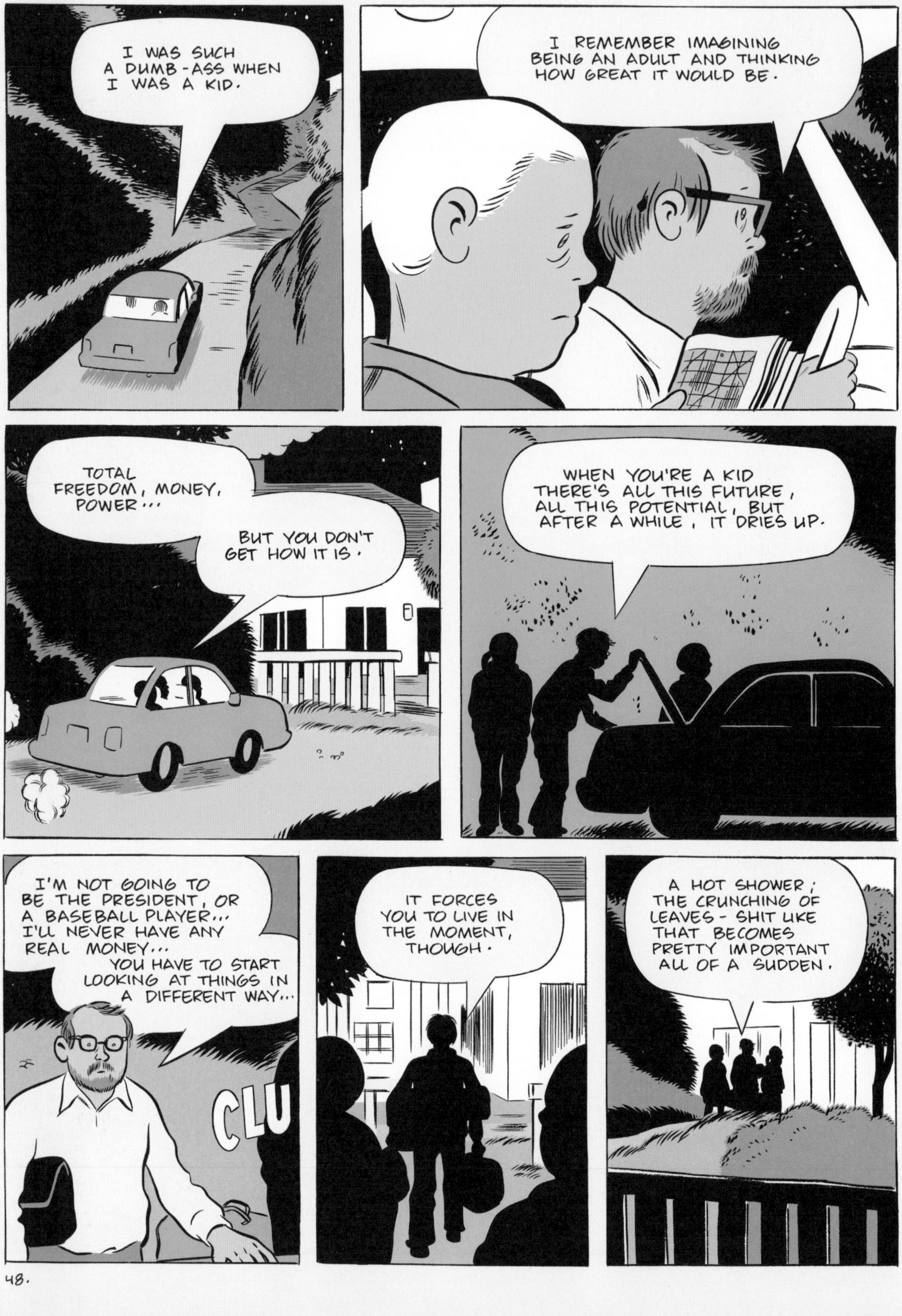
I WAS SUCH A DUMB-ASS WHEN I WAS A KID.
I REMEMBER IMAGINING BEING AN ADULT AND THINKING HOW GREAT IT WOULD BE.
TOTAL FREEDOM, MONEY, POWER...
BUT YOU DON'T GET HOW IT IS.
WHEN YOU'RE A KID THERE'S ALL THIS FUTURE, ALL THIS POTENTIAL, BUT AFTER A WHILE, IT DRIES UP.
I'M NOT GOING TO BE THE PRESIDENT, OR A BASEBALL PLAYER... I'LL NEVER HAVE ANY REAL MONEY...
YOU HAVE TO START LOOKING AT THINGS IN A DIFFERENT WAY...
CLU
IT FORCES YOU TO LIVE IN THE MOMENT, THOUGH.
A HOT SHOWER; THE CRUNCHING OF LEAVES - SHIT LIKE THAT BECOMES PRETTY IMPORTANT ALL OF A SUDDEN.

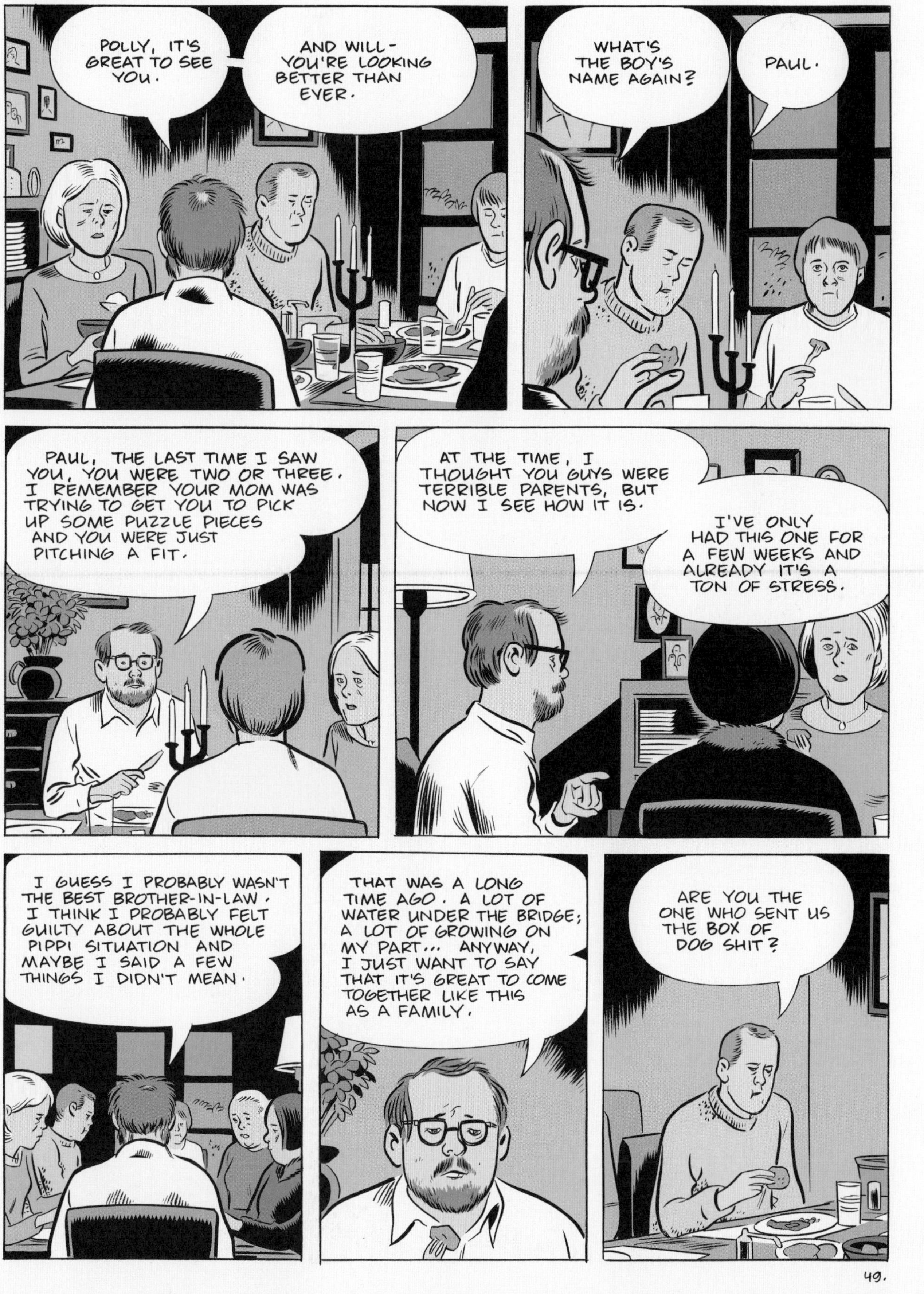
POLLY, IT'S GREAT TO SEE YOU.
AND WILL- YOU'RE LOOKING BETTER THAN EVER.
WHAT'S THE BOY'S NAME AGAIN?
PAUL.
PAUL, THE LAST TIME I SAW YOU, YOU WERE TWO OR THREE. I REMEMBER YOUR MOM WAS TRYING TO GET YOU TO PICK UP SOME PUZZLE PIECES AND YOU WERE JUST PITCHING A FIT.
AT THE TIME, I THOUGHT YOU GUYS WERE TERRIBLE PARENTS, BUT NOW I SEE HOW IT IS.
I'VE ONLY HAD THIS ONE FOR A FEW WEEKS AND ALREADY IT'S A TON OF STRESS.
I GUESS I PROBABLY WASN'T THE BEST BROTHER-IN-LAW. I THINK I PROBABLY FELT GUILTY ABOUT THE WHOLE PIPPI SITUATION AND MAYBE I SAID A FEW THINGS I DIDN'T MEAN.
THAT WAS A LONG TIME AGO. A LOT OF WATER UNDER THE BRIDGE; A LOT OF GROWING ON MY PART... ANYWAY, I JUST WANT TO SAY THAT IT'S GREAT TO COME TOGETHER LIKE THIS AS A FAMILY.
ARE YOU THE ONE WHO SENT US THE BOX OF DOG SHIT?

FIRESIDE CHAT

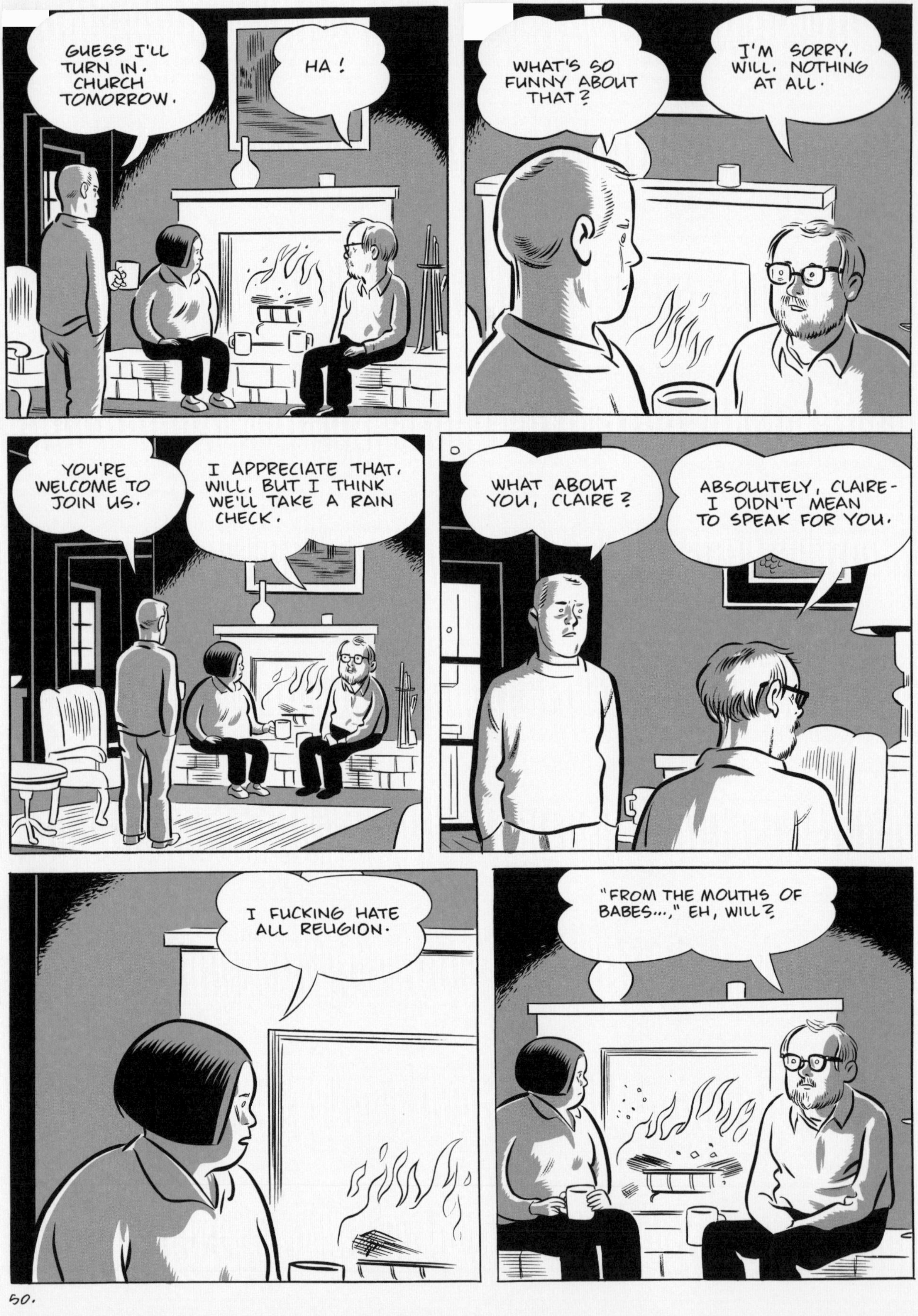

GUESS I'LL TURN IN. CHURCH TOMORROW.
HA!
WHAT'S SO FUNNY ABOUT THAT?
I'M SORRY, WILL. NOTHING AT ALL.
YOU'RE WELCOME TO JOIN US.
I APPRECIATE THAT, WILL, BUT I THINK WE'LL TAKE A RAIN CHECK.
WHAT ABOUT YOU, CLAIRE?
ABSOLUTELY, CLAIRE- I DIDN'T MEAN TO SPEAK FOR YOU.
I FUCKING HATE ALL RELIGION.
"FROM THE MOUTHS OF BABES...," EH, WILL?

PURE BLISS

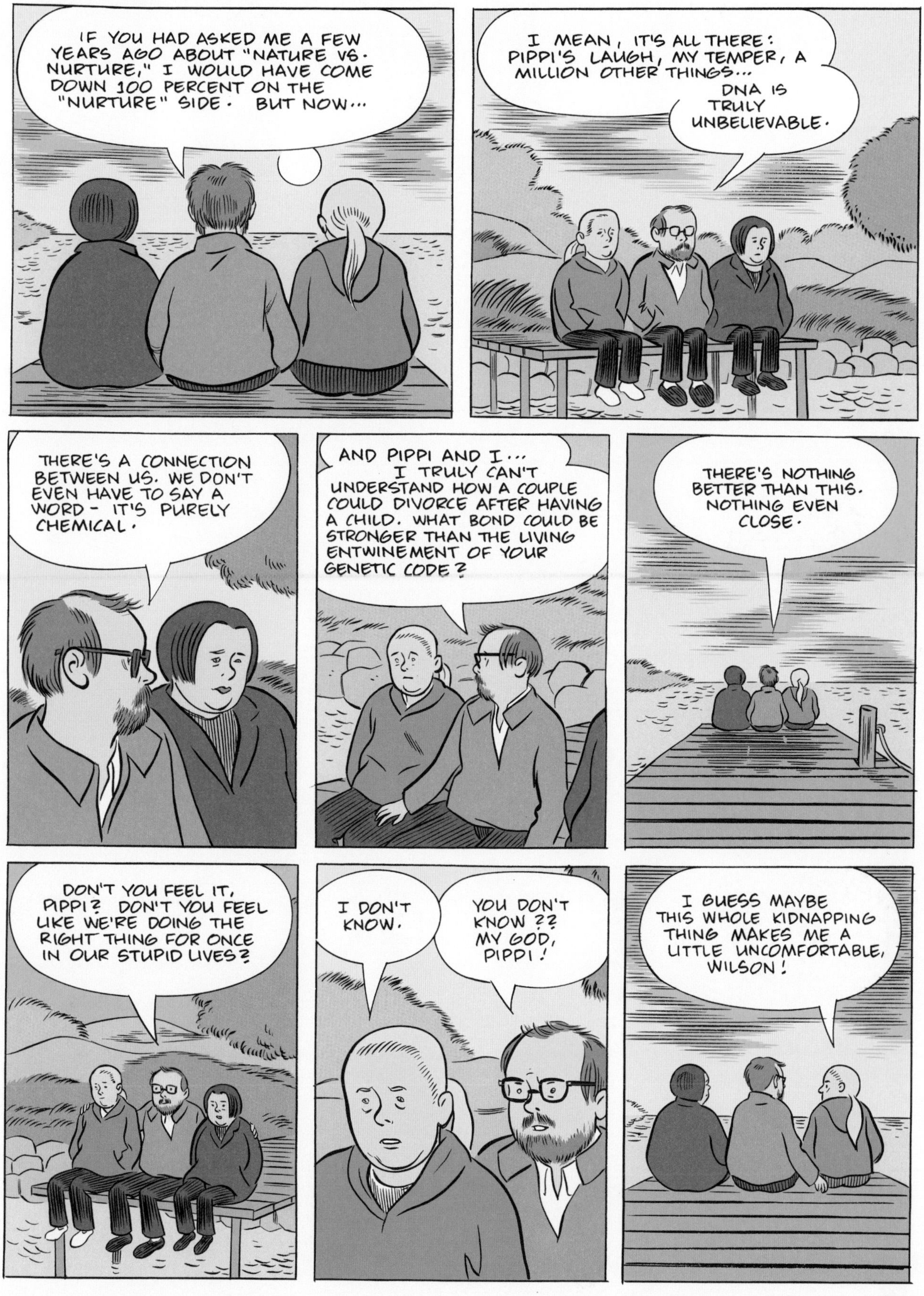

IF YOU HAD ASKED ME A FEW YEARS AGO ABOUT "NATURE VS. NURTURE," I WOULD HAVE COME DOWN 100 PERCENT ON THE "NURTURE" SIDE. BUT NOW...
I MEAN, IT'S ALL THERE: PIPPI'S LAUGH, MY TEMPER, A MILLION OTHER THINGS...
DNA IS TRULY UNBELIEVABLE.
THERE'S A CONNECTION BETWEEN US. WE DON'T EVEN HAVE TO SAY A WORD - IT'S PURELY CHEMICAL.
AND PIPPI AND I... I TRULY CAN'T UNDERSTAND HOW A COUPLE COULD DIVORCE AFTER HAVING A CHILD. WHAT BOND COULD BE STRONGER THAN THE LIVING ENTWINEMENT OF YOUR GENETIC CODE?
THERE'S NOTHING BETTER THAN THIS. NOTHING EVEN CLOSE.
DON'T YOU FEEL IT, PIPPI? DON'T YOU FEEL LIKE WE'RE DOING THE RIGHT THING FOR ONCE IN OUR STUPID LIVES?
I DON'T KNOW.
YOU DON'T KNOW?? MY GOD, PIPPI!
I GUESS MAYBE THIS WHOLE KIDNAPPING THING MAKES ME A LITTLE UNCOMFORTABLE, WILSON!

EMPTY POOL

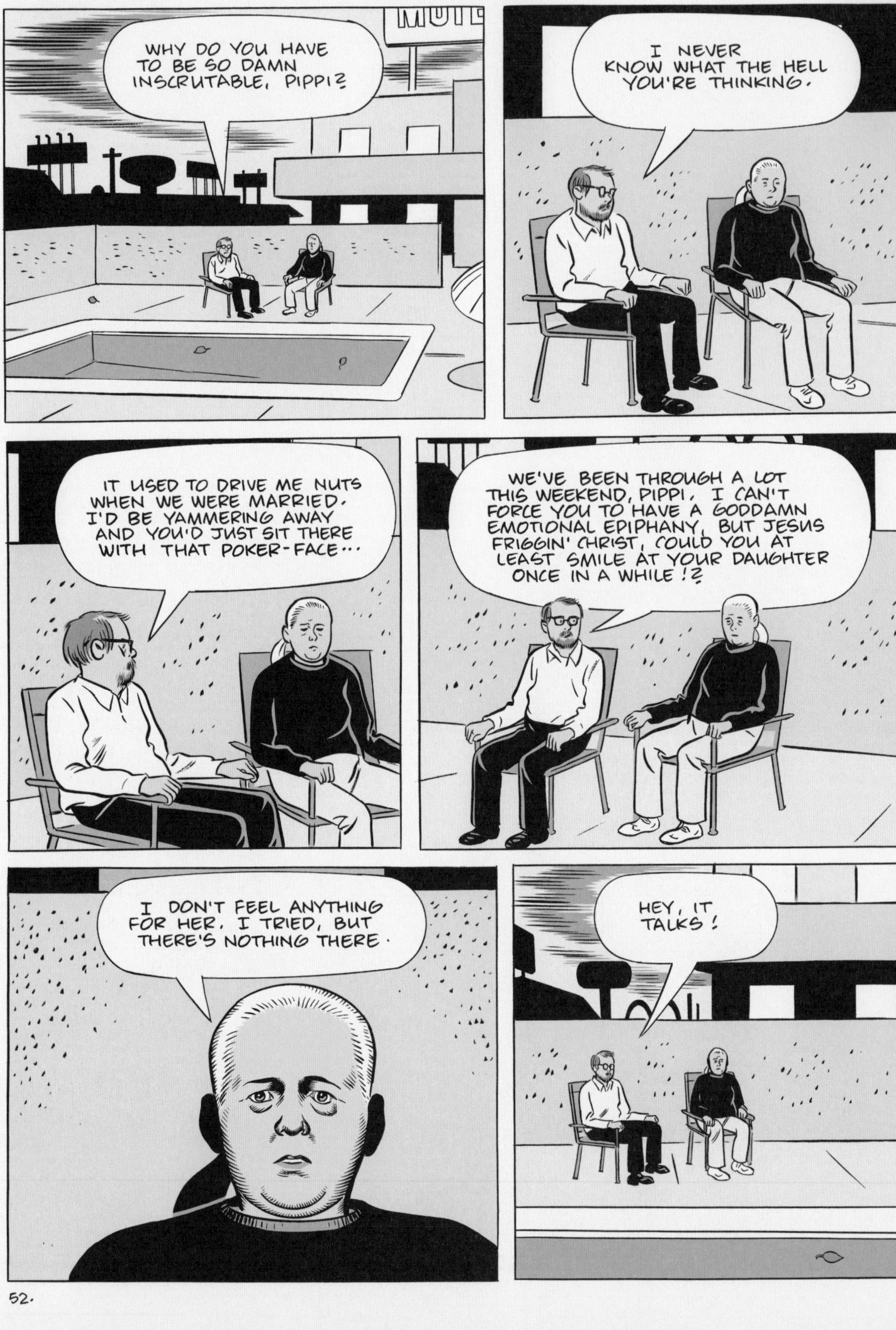
WHY DO YOU HAVE TO BE SO DAMN INSCRUTABLE, PIPPI?
I NEVER KNOW WHAT THE HELL YOU'RE THINKING.
IT USED TO DRIVE ME NUTS WHEN WE WERE MARRIED. I'D BE YAMMERING AWAY AND YOU'D JUST SIT THERE WITH THAT POKER-FACE...
WE'VE BEEN THROUGH A LOT THIS WEEKEND, PIPPI. I CAN'T FORCE YOU TO HAVE A GODDAMN EMOTIONAL EPIPHANY, BUT JESUS FRIGGIN' CHRIST, COULD YOU AT LEAST SMILE AT YOUR DAUGHTER ONCE IN A WHILE!?
I DON'T FEEL ANYTHING FOR HER. I TRIED, BUT THERE'S NOTHING THERE.
HEY, IT TALKS!

FUCKING BITCH

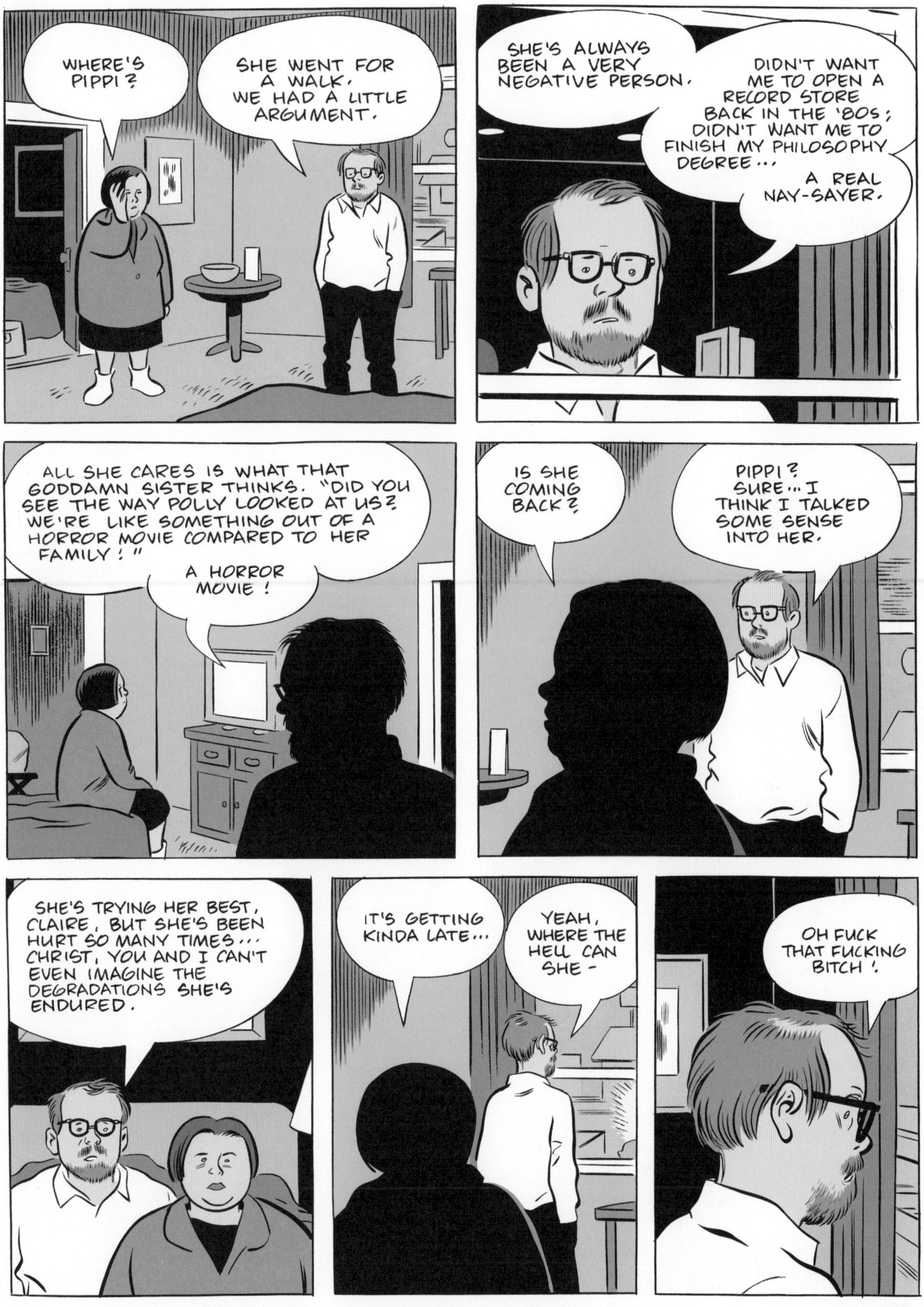
WHERE'S PIPPI?
SHE WENT FOR A WALK. WE HAD A LITTLE ARGUMENT.
SHE'S ALWAYS BEEN A VERY NEGATIVE PERSON.
DIDN'T WANT ME TO OPEN A RECORD STORE BACK IN THE '80S; DIDN'T WANT ME TO FINISH MY PHILOSOPHY DEGREE...
A REAL NAY-SAYER.
ALL SHE CARES IS WHAT THAT GODDAMN SISTER THINKS. "DID YOU SEE THE WAY POLLY LOOKED AT US? WE'RE LIKE SOMETHING OUT OF A HORROR MOVIE COMPARED TO HER FAMILY!"
A HORROR MOVIE!
IS SHE COMING BACK?
PIPPI? SURE... I THINK I TALKED SOME SENSE INTO HER.
SHE'S TRYING HER BEST, CLAIRE, BUT SHE'S BEEN HURT SO MANY TIMES... CHRIST, YOU AND I CAN'T EVEN IMAGINE THE DEGRADATIONS SHE'S ENDURED.
IT'S GETTING KINDA LATE...
YEAH, WHERE THE HELL CAN SHE -
OH FUCK THAT FUCKING BITCH!

BELIEVE IT OR NOT, I ACTUALLY USED TO KIND-OF FANTASIZE ABOUT GOING TO PRISON.
IT SEEMS LIKE A GOOD PLACE TO DO SOME SERIOUS THINKING. MAYBE READ SOME BOOKS, DO SOME WRITING... COLLECT YOUR THOUGHTS, Y'KNOW?
I ALWAYS WANTED TO READ THE RUSSIANS - TURGENEV, GOGOL; THOSE GUYS. DO THEY HAVE THAT STUFF IN THE LIBRARY? PROBABLY NOT...
I'M READY TO GET OFF THE MEDIA TREADMILL FOR A WHILE. POLITICS, SPORTS, CELEBRITY GOSSIP; ALL OF IT! LET'S TAKE A DAMN BREAK!
I MEAN, I LOVE BASEBALL AS MUCH AS THE NEXT GUY, BUT CAN'T WE HAVE A REST ONCE IN A WHILE? THE WORLD SERIES ENDS AND A MONTH LATER WE'RE BACK IN SPRING TRAINING!
YOU SHUT UP FO' I GON' TURN YO' ASSHO' INTO A PUSSY!

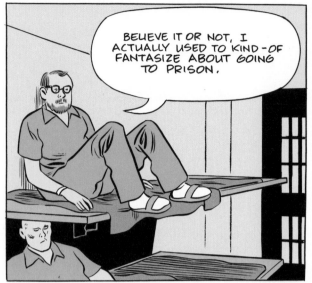

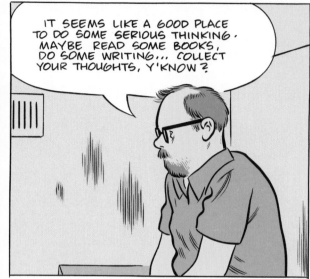

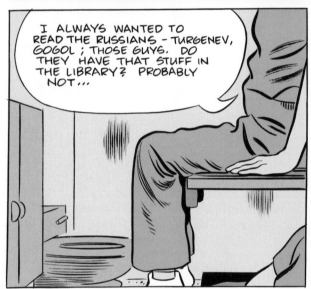

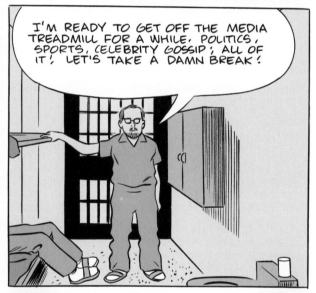

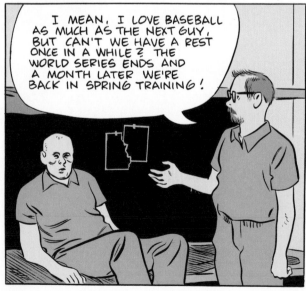

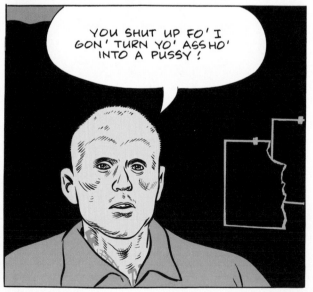

BIBLE STUDY

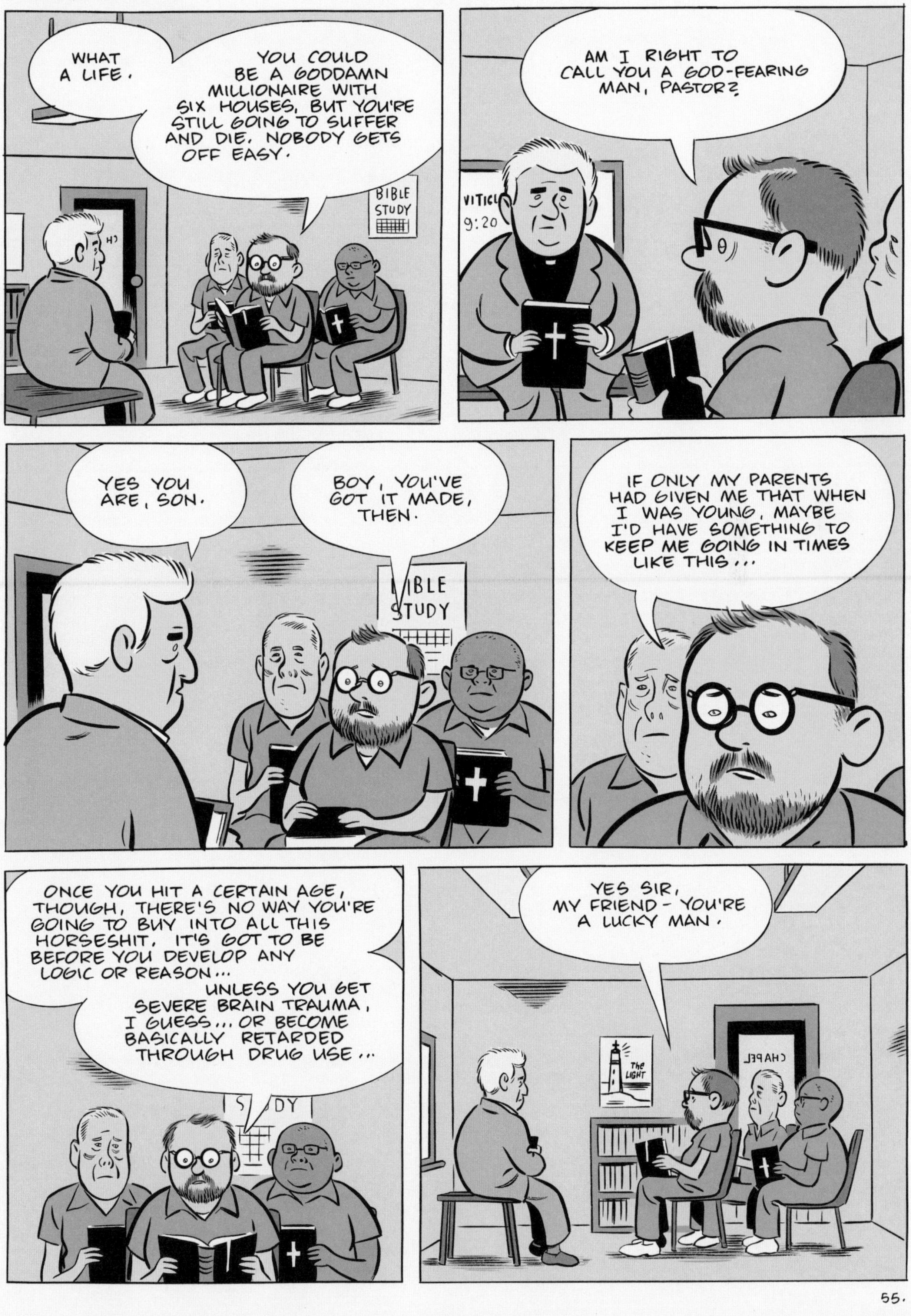
WHAT A LIFE.
YOU COULD BE A GODDAMN MILLIONAIRE WITH SIX HOUSES, BUT YOU'RE STILL GOING TO SUFFER AND DIE. NOBODY GETS OFF EASY.
BIBLE STUDY
AM I RIGHT TO CALL YOU A GOD-FEARING MAN, PASTOR?
VITICU
9:20
YES YOU ARE, SON.
BOY, YOU'VE GOT IT MADE, THEN.
BIBLE STUDY
IF ONLY MY PARENTS HAD GIVEN ME THAT WHEN I WAS YOUNG, MAYBE I'D HAVE SOMETHING TO KEEP ME GOING IN TIMES LIKE THIS...
ONCE YOU HIT A CERTAIN AGE, THOUGH, THERE'S NO WAY YOU'RE GOING TO BUY INTO ALL THIS HORSESHIT. IT'S GOT TO BE BEFORE YOU DEVELOP ANY LOGIC OR REASON...
UNLESS YOU GET SEVERE BRAIN TRAUMA, I GUESS... OR BECOME BASICALLY RETARDED THROUGH DRUG USE...
YES SIR, MY FRIEND - YOU'RE A LUCKY MAN.
The LIGHT
CHAPEL

NEW CELLMATE

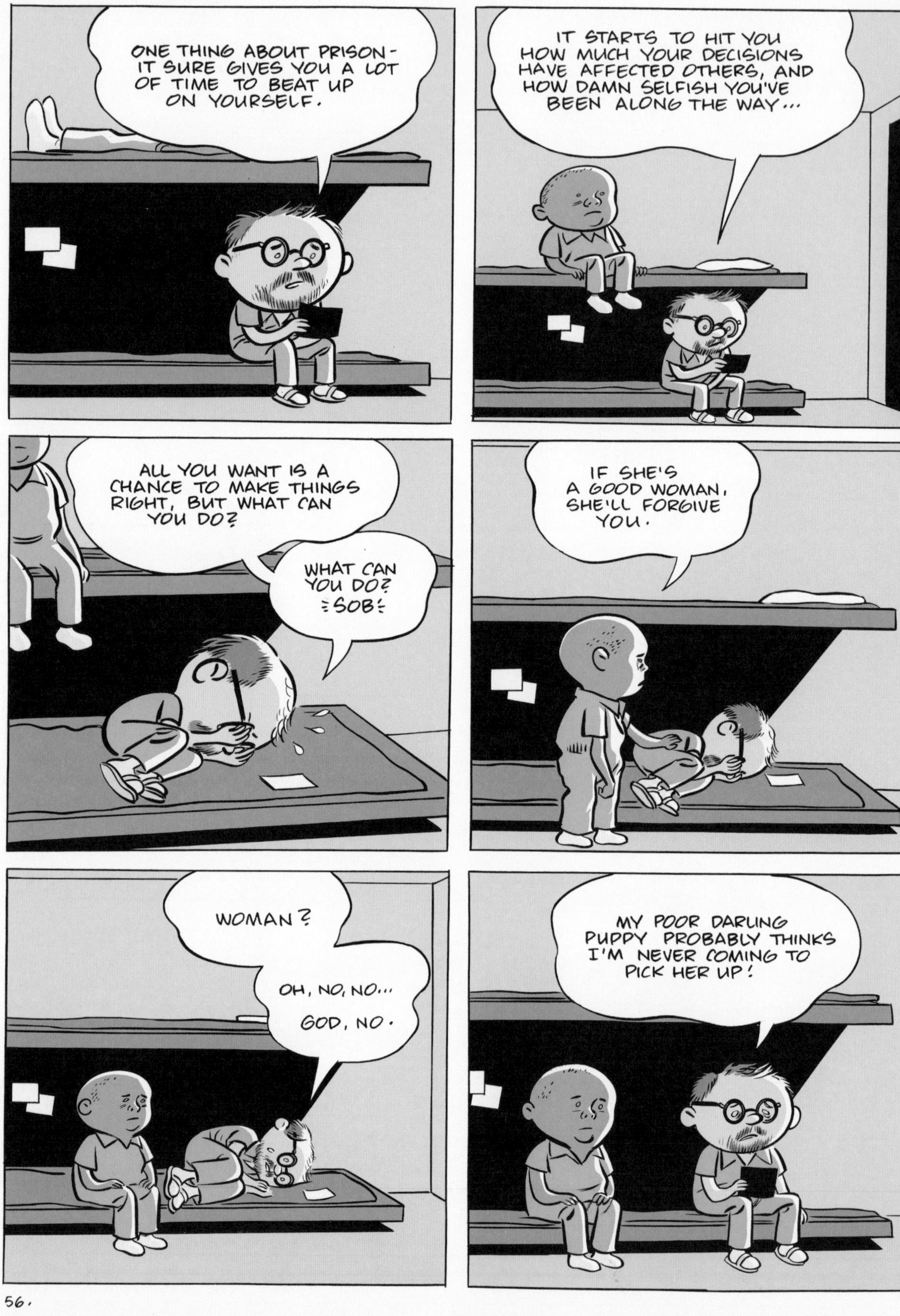

ONE THING ABOUT PRISON- IT SURE GIVES YOU A LOT OF TIME TO BEAT UP ON YOURSELF.
IT STARTS TO HIT YOU HOW MUCH YOUR DECISIONS HAVE AFFECTED OTHERS, AND HOW DAMN SELFISH YOU'VE BEEN ALONG THE WAY...
ALL YOU WANT IS A CHANCE TO MAKE THINGS RIGHT, BUT WHAT CAN YOU DO?
WHAT CAN YOU DO? SOB
IF SHE'S A GOOD WOMAN, SHE'LL FORGIVE YOU.
WOMAN?
OH, NO, NO...
GOD, NO.
MY POOR DARLING PUPPY PROBABLY THINKS I'M NEVER COMING TO PICK HER UP!

PHONE PRIVELEGES

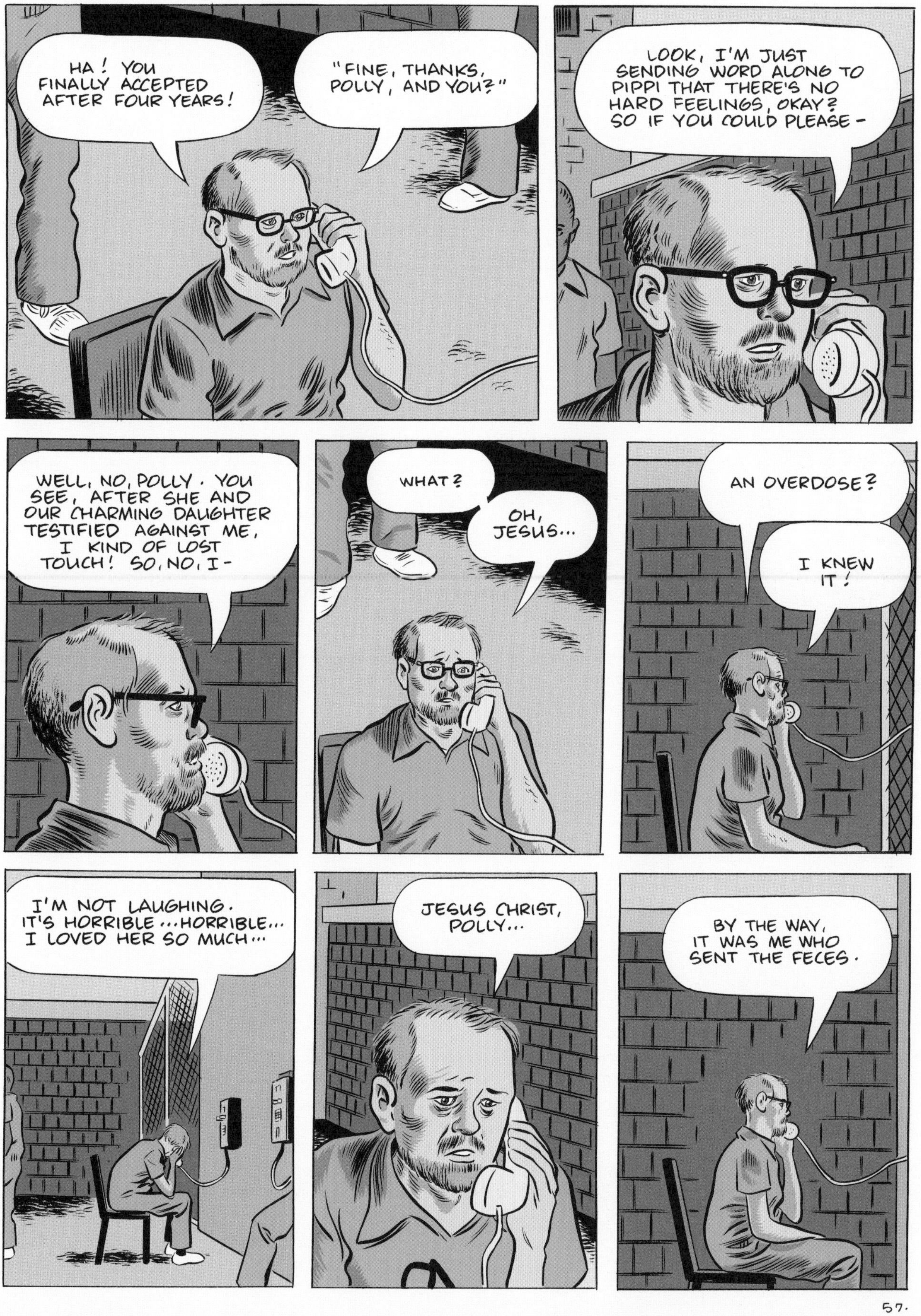
HA! YOU FINALLY ACCEPTED AFTER FOUR YEARS!
"FINE, THANKS, POLLY, AND YOU?"
LOOK, I'M JUST SENDING WORD ALONG TO PIPPI THAT THERE'S NO HARD FEELINGS, OKAY? SO IF YOU COULD PLEASE -
WELL, NO, POLLY. YOU SEE, AFTER SHE AND OUR CHARMING DAUGHTER TESTIFIED AGAINST ME, I KIND OF LOST TOUCH! SO, NO, I -
WHAT?
OH, JESUS...
AN OVERDOSE?
I KNEW IT!
I'M NOT LAUGHING. IT'S HORRIBLE...HORRIBLE... I LOVED HER SO MUCH...
JESUS CHRIST, POLLY...
BY THE WAY, IT WAS ME WHO SENT THE FECES.

ICICLE

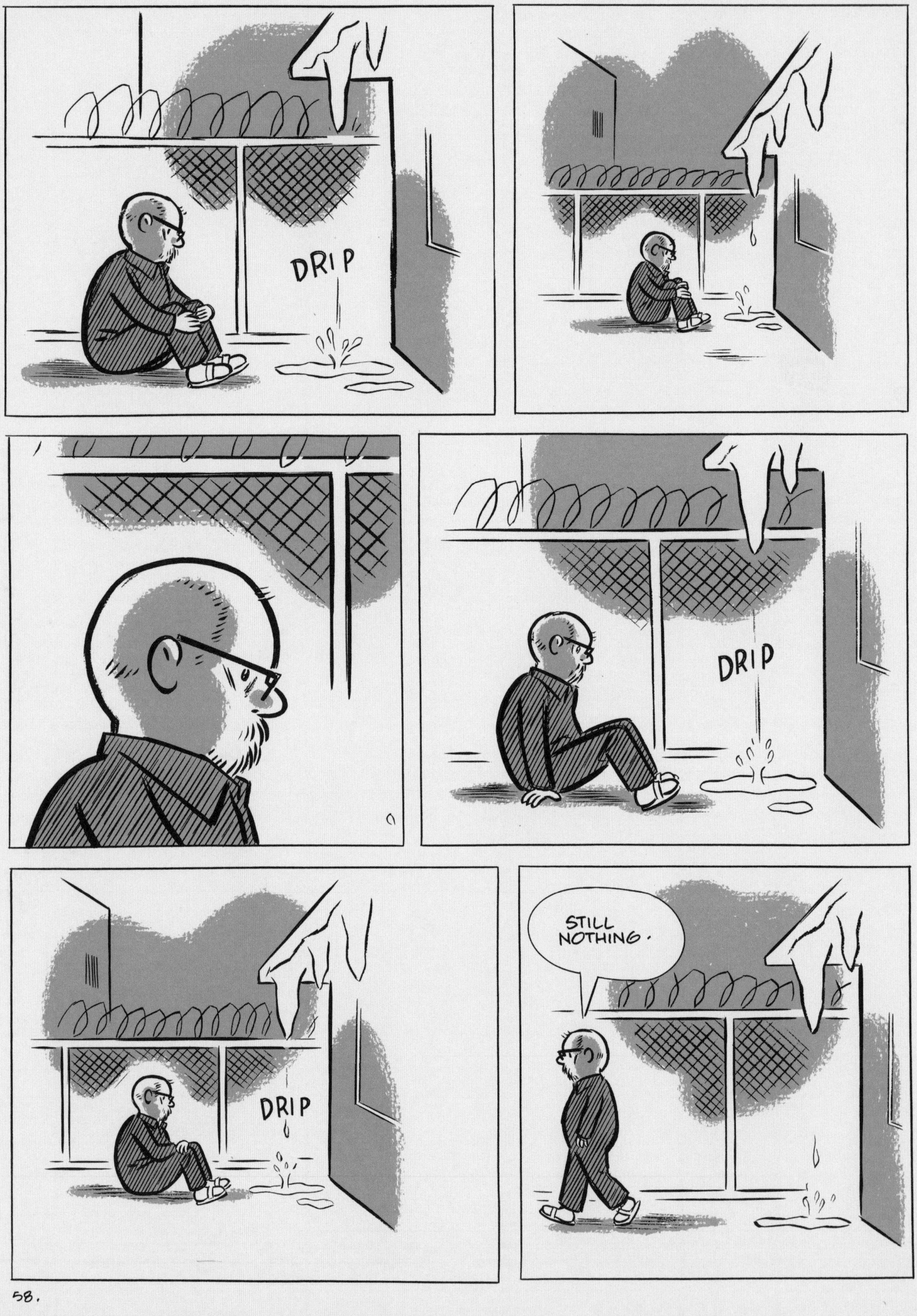
DRIP
DRIP
DRIP
STILL NOTHING.

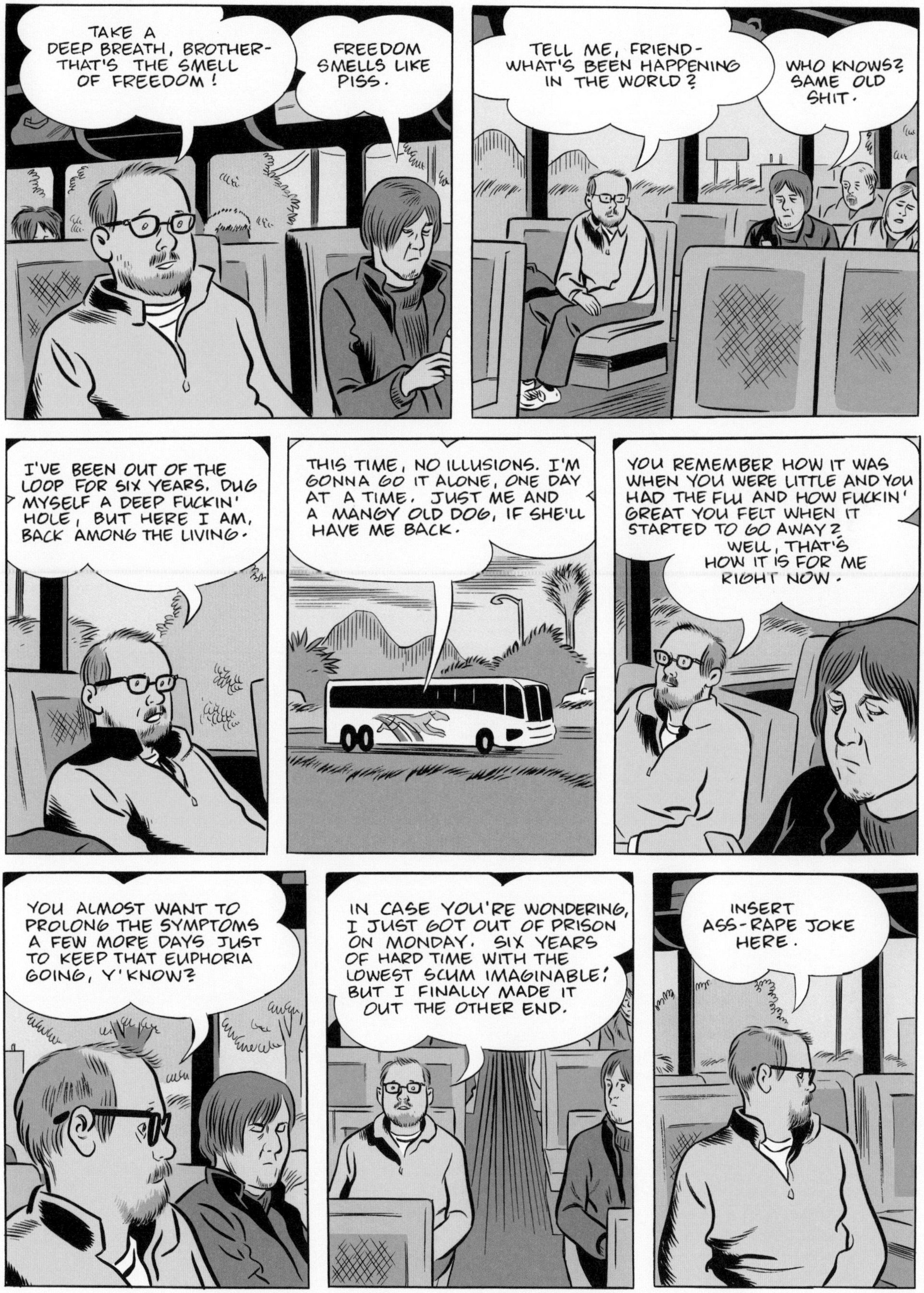
TAKE A DEEP BREATH, BROTHER- THAT'S THE SMELL OF FREEDOM!
FREEDOM SMELLS LIKE PISS.
TELL ME, FRIEND- WHAT'S BEEN HAPPENING IN THE WORLD?
WHO KNOWS? SAME OLD SHIT.
I'VE BEEN OUT OF THE LOOP FOR SIX YEARS. DUG MYSELF A DEEP FUCKIN' HOLE, BUT HERE I AM, BACK AMONG THE LIVING.
THIS TIME, NO ILLUSIONS. I'M GONNA GO IT ALONE, ONE DAY AT A TIME. JUST ME AND A MANGY OLD DOG, IF SHE'LL HAVE ME BACK.
YOU REMEMBER HOW IT WAS WHEN YOU WERE LITTLE AND YOU HAD THE FLU AND HOW FUCKIN' GREAT YOU FELT WHEN IT STARTED TO GO AWAY? WELL, THAT'S HOW IT IS FOR ME RIGHT NOW.
YOU ALMOST WANT TO PROLONG THE SYMPTOMS A FEW MORE DAYS JUST TO KEEP THAT EUPHORIA GOING, Y'KNOW?
IN CASE YOU'RE WONDERING, I JUST GOT OUT OF PRISON ON MONDAY. SIX YEARS OF HARD TIME WITH THE LOWEST SCUM IMAGINABLE; BUT I FINALLY MADE IT OUT THE OTHER END.
INSERT ASS-RAPE JOKE HERE.

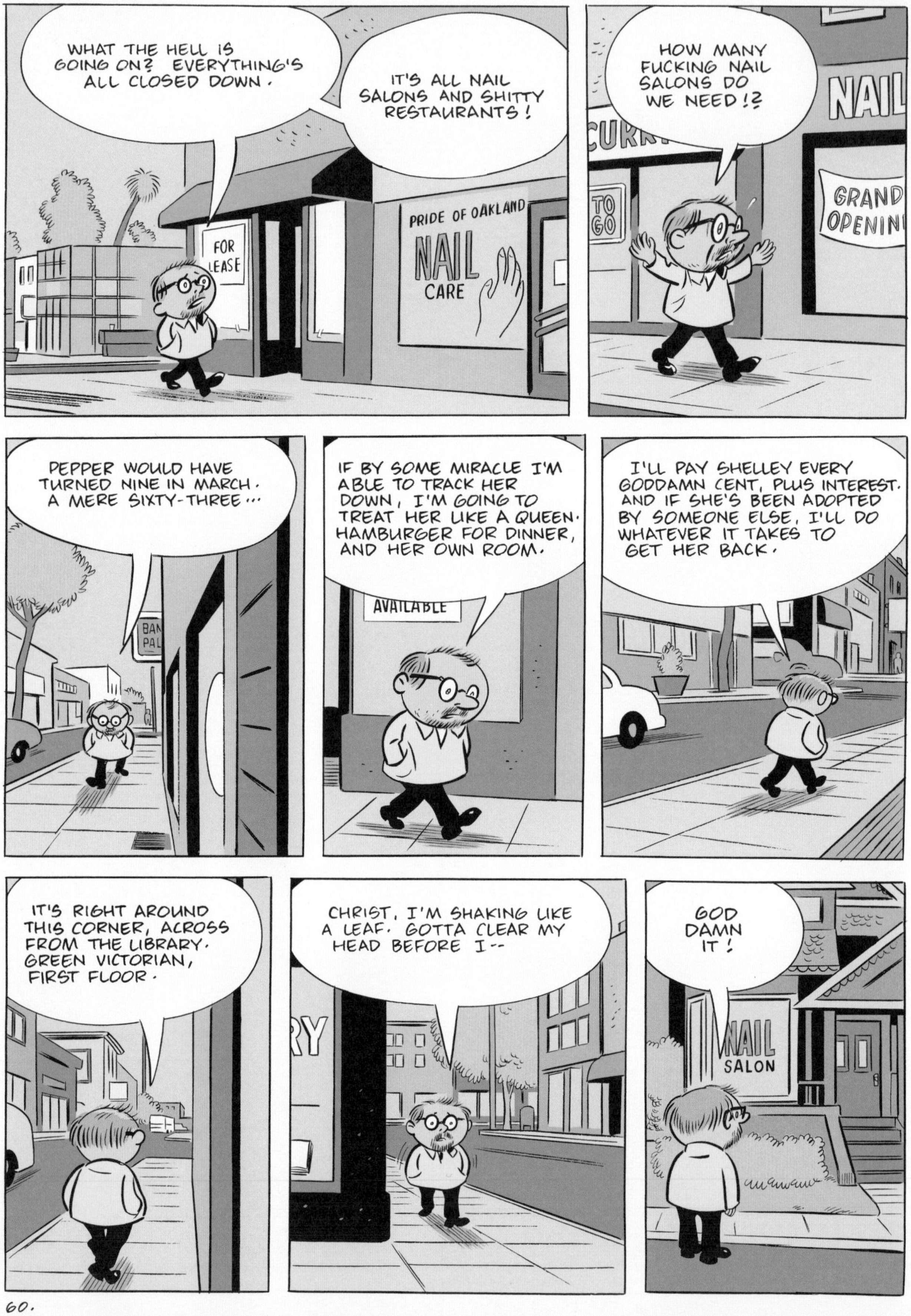
WHAT THE HELL IS GOING ON? EVERYTHING'S ALL CLOSED DOWN.
IT'S ALL NAIL SALONS AND SHITTY RESTAURANTS!
FOR LEASE
PRIDE OF OAKLAND
NAIL CARE
HOW MANY FUCKING NAIL SALONS DO WE NEED!?
TO GO
NAIL
GRAND OPENIN
PEPPER WOULD HAVE TURNED NINE IN MARCH. A MERE SIXTY-THREE...
IF BY SOME MIRACLE I'M ABLE TO TRACK HER DOWN, I'M GOING TO TREAT HER LIKE A QUEEN. HAMBURGER FOR DINNER, AND HER OWN ROOM.
AVAILABLE
I'LL PAY SHELLEY EVERY GODDAMN CENT, PLUS INTEREST. AND IF SHE'S BEEN ADOPTED BY SOMEONE ELSE, I'LL DO WHATEVER IT TAKES TO GET HER BACK.
IT'S RIGHT AROUND THIS CORNER, ACROSS FROM THE LIBRARY. GREEN VICTORIAN, FIRST FLOOR.
CHRIST, I'M SHAKING LIKE A LEAF. GOTTA CLEAR MY HEAD BEFORE I--
GOD DAMN IT!
NAIL SALON

SHELLEY'S NEW CAREER

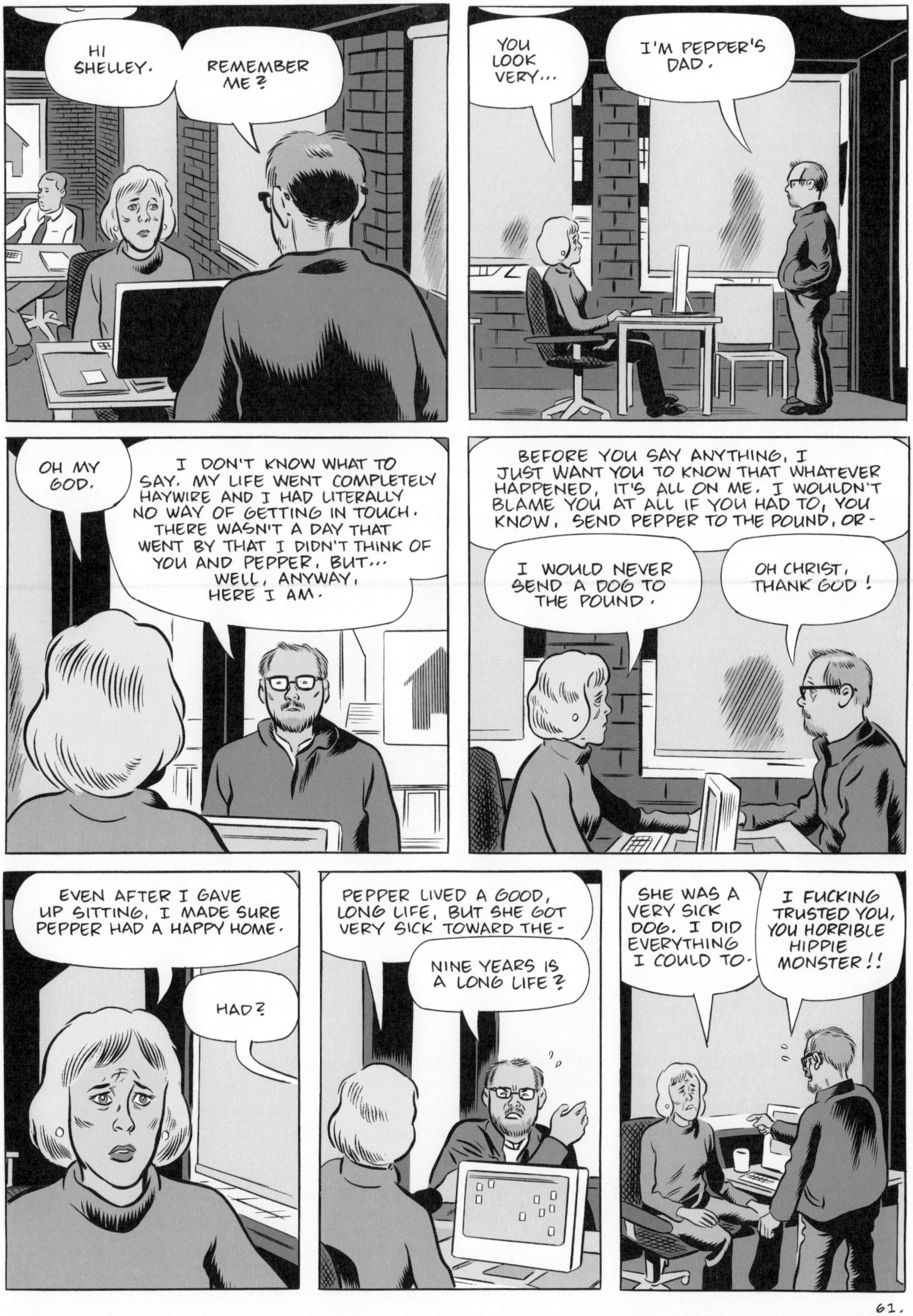
HI SHELLEY.
REMEMBER ME?
YOU LOOK VERY...
I'M PEPPER'S DAD.
OH MY GOD.
I DON'T KNOW WHAT TO SAY. MY LIFE WENT COMPLETELY HAYWIRE AND I HAD LITERALLY NO WAY OF GETTING IN TOUCH. THERE WASN'T A DAY THAT WENT BY THAT I DIDN'T THINK OF YOU AND PEPPER. BUT... WELL, ANYWAY, HERE I AM.
BEFORE YOU SAY ANYTHING, I JUST WANT YOU TO KNOW THAT WHATEVER HAPPENED, IT'S ALL ON ME. I WOULDN'T BLAME YOU AT ALL IF YOU HAD TO, YOU KNOW, SEND PEPPER TO THE POUND, OR-
I WOULD NEVER SEND A DOG TO THE POUND.
OH CHRIST, THANK GOD!
EVEN AFTER I GAVE UP SITTING, I MADE SURE PEPPER HAD A HAPPY HOME.
HAD?
PEPPER LIVED A GOOD, LONG LIFE, BUT SHE GOT VERY SICK TOWARD THE-
NINE YEARS IS A LONG LIFE?
SHE WAS A VERY SICK DOG. I DID EVERYTHING I COULD TO-
I FUCKING TRUSTED YOU, YOU HORRIBLE HIPPIE MONSTER!!

THE LAST TIME

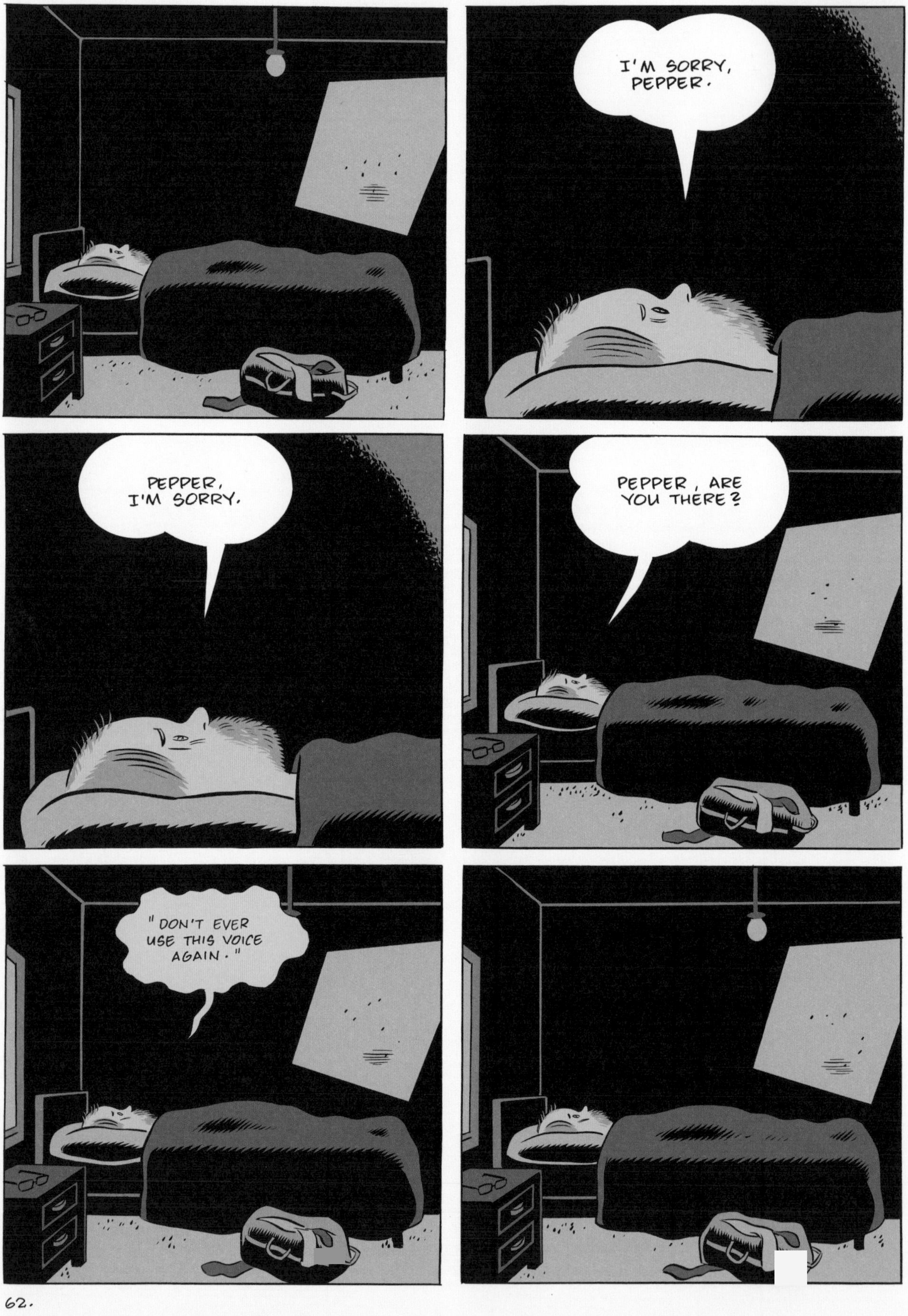
I'M SORRY, PEPPER.
PEPPER, I'M SORRY.
PEPPER, ARE YOU THERE?
"DON'T EVER USE THIS VOICE AGAIN."

EULOGY

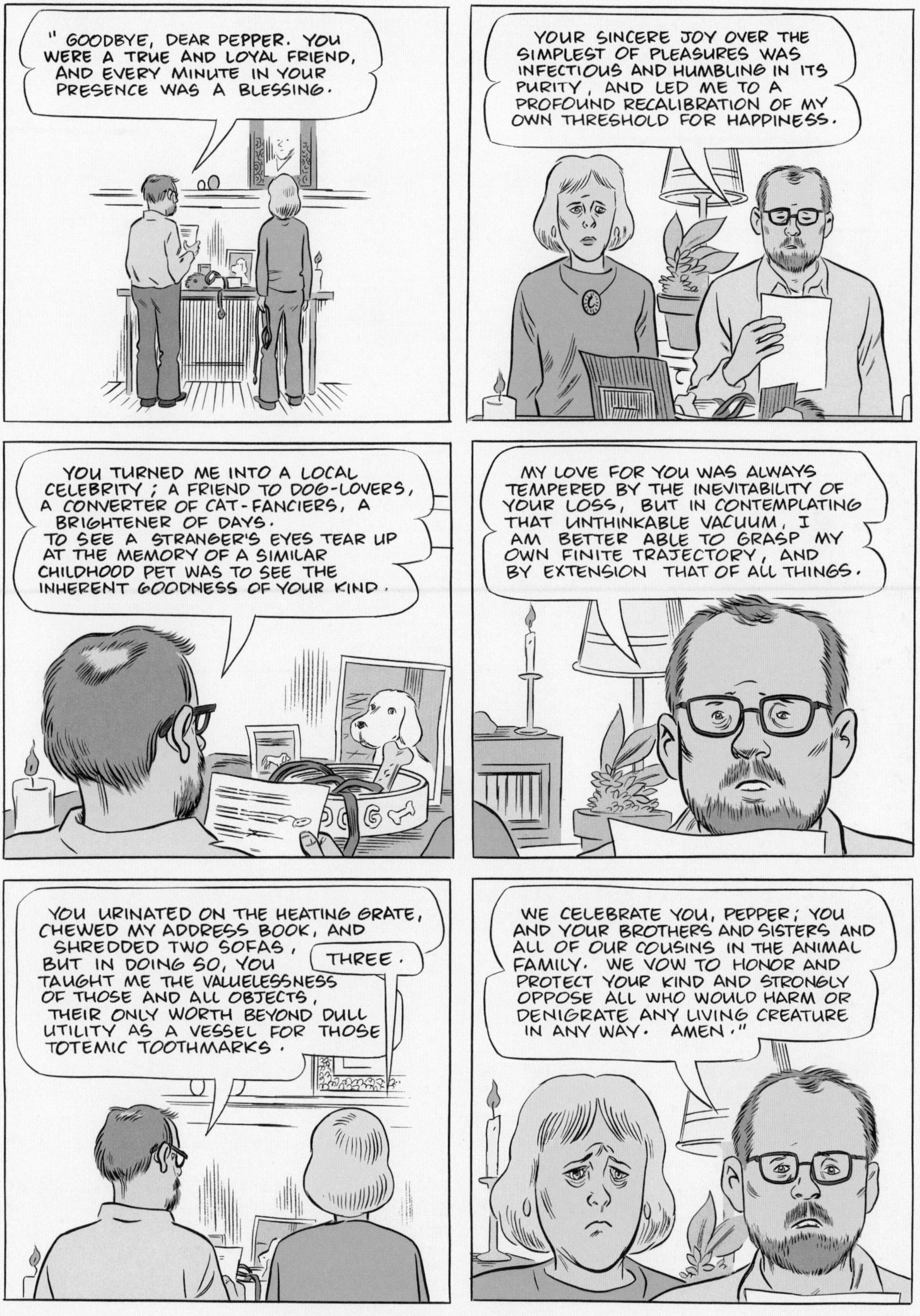
" GOODBYE, DEAR PEPPER. YOU WERE A TRUE AND LOYAL FRIEND, AND EVERY MINUTE IN YOUR PRESENCE WAS A BLESSING.
YOUR SINCERE JOY OVER THE SIMPLEST OF PLEASURES WAS INFECTIOUS AND HUMBLING IN ITS PURITY, AND LED ME TO A PROFOUND RECALIBRATION OF MY OWN THRESHOLD FOR HAPPINESS.
YOU TURNED ME INTO A LOCAL CELEBRITY ; A FRIEND TO DOG-LOVERS, A CONVERTER OF CAT-FANCIERS, A BRIGHTENER OF DAYS. TO SEE A STRANGER'S EYES TEAR UP AT THE MEMORY OF A SIMILAR CHILDHOOD PET WAS TO SEE THE INHERENT GOODNESS OF YOUR KIND.
MY LOVE FOR YOU WAS ALWAYS TEMPERED BY THE INEVITABILITY OF YOUR LOSS, BUT IN CONTEMPLATING THAT UNTHINKABLE VACUUM, I AM BETTER ABLE TO GRASP MY OWN FINITE TRAJECTORY, AND BY EXTENSION THAT OF ALL THINGS.
YOU URINATED ON THE HEATING GRATE, CHEWED MY ADDRESS BOOK, AND SHREDDED TWO SOFAS,
THREE.
BUT IN DOING SO, YOU TAUGHT ME THE VALUELESSNESS OF THOSE AND ALL OBJECTS, THEIR ONLY WORTH BEYOND DULL UTILITY AS A VESSEL FOR THOSE TOTEMIC TOOTHMARKS.
WE CELEBRATE YOU, PEPPER; YOU AND YOUR BROTHERS AND SISTERS AND ALL OF OUR COUSINS IN THE ANIMAL FAMILY. WE VOW TO HONOR AND PROTECT YOUR KIND AND STRONGLY OPPOSE ALL WHO WOULD HARM OR DENIGRATE ANY LIVING CREATURE IN ANY WAY. AMEN."

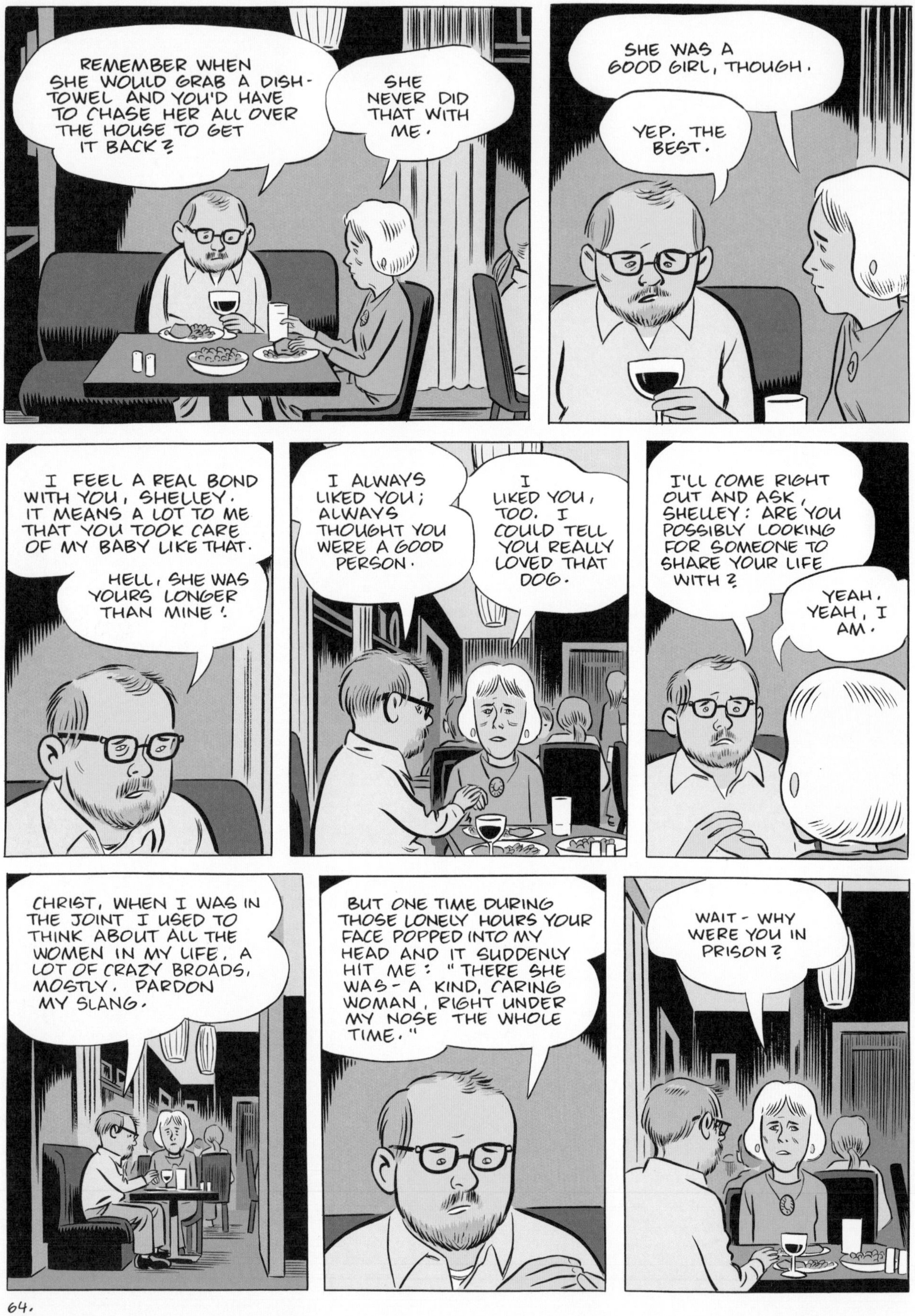
REMEMBER WHEN SHE WOULD GRAB A DISH-TOWEL AND YOU'D HAVE TO CHASE HER ALL OVER THE HOUSE TO GET IT BACK?
SHE NEVER DID THAT WITH ME.
SHE WAS A GOOD GIRL, THOUGH.
YEP. THE BEST.
I FEEL A REAL BOND WITH YOU, SHELLEY. IT MEANS A LOT TO ME THAT YOU TOOK CARE OF MY BABY LIKE THAT.
HELL, SHE WAS YOURS LONGER THAN MINE!
I ALWAYS LIKED YOU; ALWAYS THOUGHT YOU WERE A GOOD PERSON.
I LIKED YOU, TOO. I COULD TELL YOU REALLY LOVED THAT DOG.
I'LL COME RIGHT OUT AND ASK, SHELLEY: ARE YOU POSSIBLY LOOKING FOR SOMEONE TO SHARE YOUR LIFE WITH?
YEAH. YEAH, I AM.
CHRIST, WHEN I WAS IN THE JOINT I USED TO THINK ABOUT ALL THE WOMEN IN MY LIFE, A LOT OF CRAZY BROADS, MOSTLY. PARDON MY SLANG.
BUT ONE TIME DURING THOSE LONELY HOURS YOUR FACE POPPED INTO MY HEAD AND IT SUDDENLY HIT ME: "THERE SHE WAS- A KIND, CARING WOMAN, RIGHT UNDER MY NOSE THE WHOLE TIME."
WAIT- WHY WERE YOU IN PRISON?

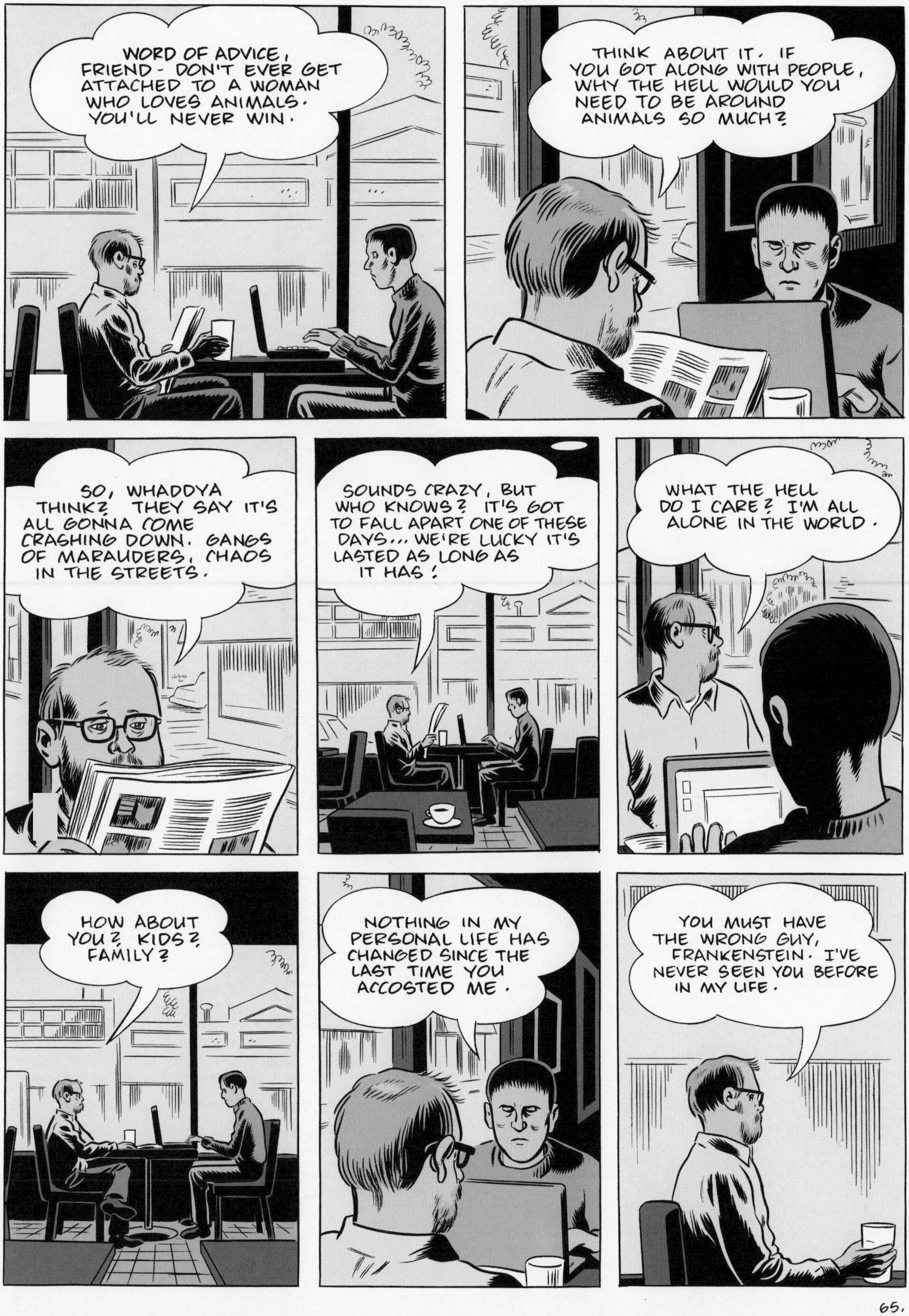
WORD OF ADVICE, FRIEND- DON'T EVER GET ATTACHED TO A WOMAN WHO LOVES ANIMALS. YOU'LL NEVER WIN.
THINK ABOUT IT. IF YOU GOT ALONG WITH PEOPLE, WHY THE HELL WOULD YOU NEED TO BE AROUND ANIMALS SO MUCH?
SO, WHADDYA THINK? THEY SAY IT'S ALL GONNA COME CRASHING DOWN. GANGS OF MARAUDERS, CHAOS IN THE STREETS.
SOUNDS CRAZY, BUT WHO KNOWS? IT'S GOT TO FALL APART ONE OF THESE DAYS... WE'RE LUCKY IT'S LASTED AS LONG AS IT HAS!
WHAT THE HELL DO I CARE? I'M ALL ALONE IN THE WORLD.
HOW ABOUT YOU? KIDS? FAMILY?
NOTHING IN MY PERSONAL LIFE HAS CHANGED SINCE THE LAST TIME YOU ACCOSTED ME.
YOU MUST HAVE THE WRONG GUY, FRANKENSTEIN. I'VE NEVER SEEN YOU BEFORE IN MY LIFE.

CRAWLING BACK

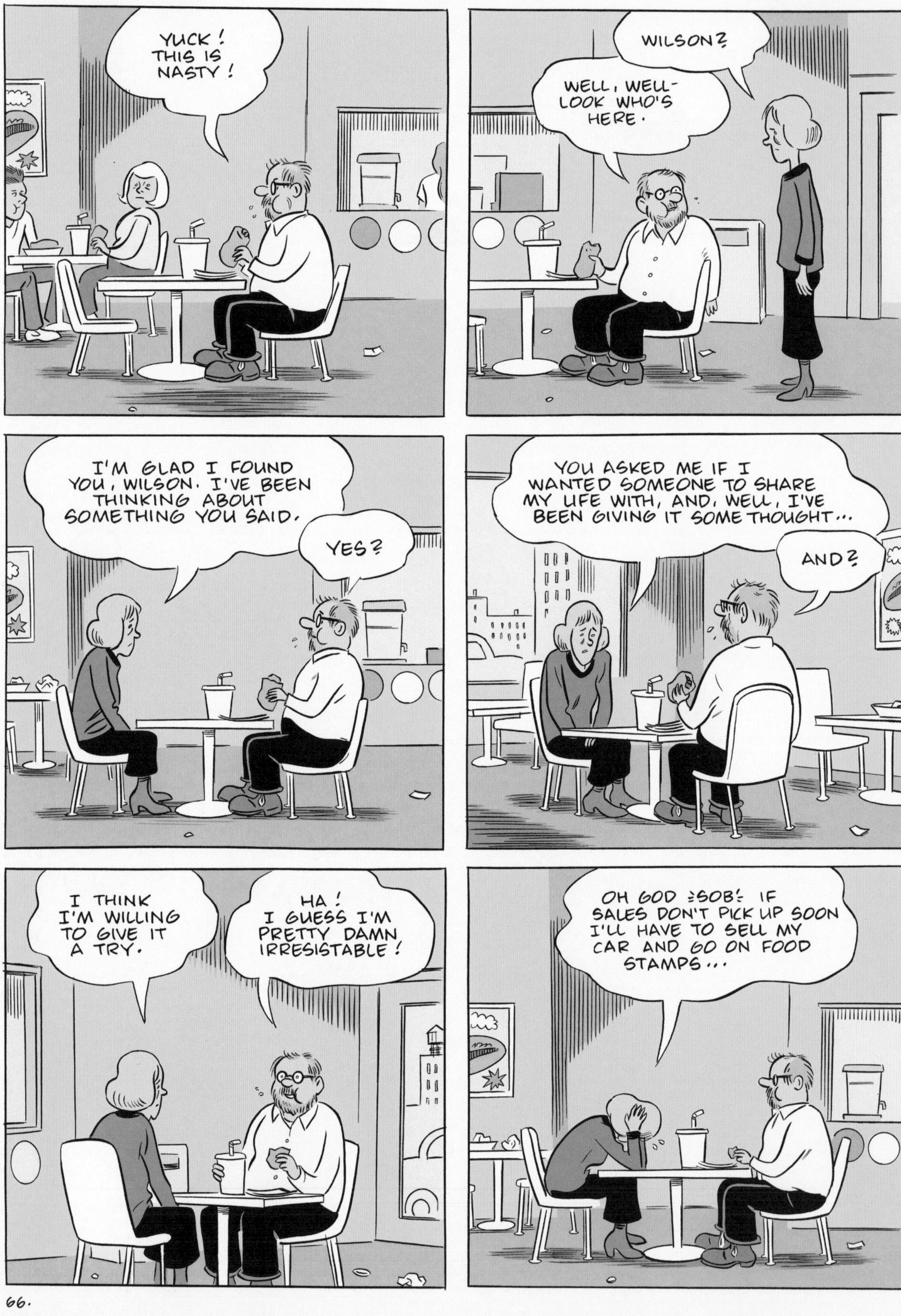
YUCK! THIS IS NASTY!
WILSON?
WELL, WELL- LOOK WHO'S HERE.
I'M GLAD I FOUND YOU, WILSON. I'VE BEEN THINKING ABOUT SOMETHING YOU SAID.
YES?
YOU ASKED ME IF I WANTED SOMEONE TO SHARE MY LIFE WITH, AND, WELL, I'VE BEEN GIVING IT SOME THOUGHT...
AND?
I THINK I'M WILLING TO GIVE IT A TRY.
HA! I GUESS I'M PRETTY DAMN IRRESISTABLE!
OH GOD =SOB= IF SALES DON'T PICK UP SOON I'LL HAVE TO SELL MY CAR AND GO ON FOOD STAMPS...

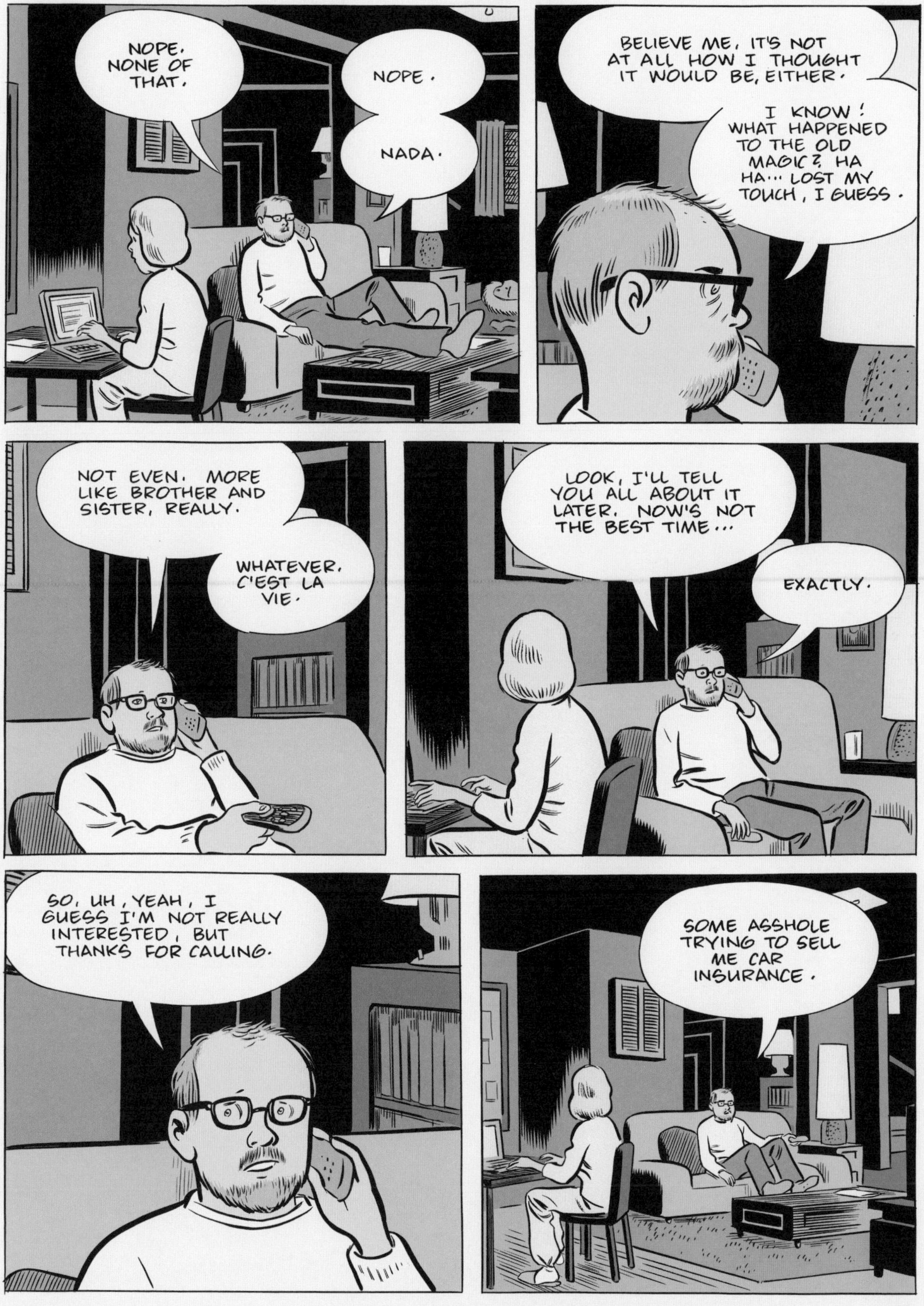
NOPE. NONE OF THAT.
NOPE.
NADA.
BELIEVE ME, IT'S NOT AT ALL HOW I THOUGHT IT WOULD BE, EITHER.
I KNOW! WHAT HAPPENED TO THE OLD MAGIC?, HA HA... LOST MY TOUCH, I GUESS.
NOT EVEN. MORE LIKE BROTHER AND SISTER, REALLY.
WHATEVER. C'EST LA VIE.
LOOK, I'LL TELL YOU ALL ABOUT IT LATER. NOW'S NOT THE BEST TIME...
EXACTLY.
SO, UH, YEAH, I GUESS I'M NOT REALLY INTERESTED, BUT THANKS FOR CALLING.
SOME ASSHOLE TRYING TO SELL ME CAR INSURANCE.

POWERBOOK

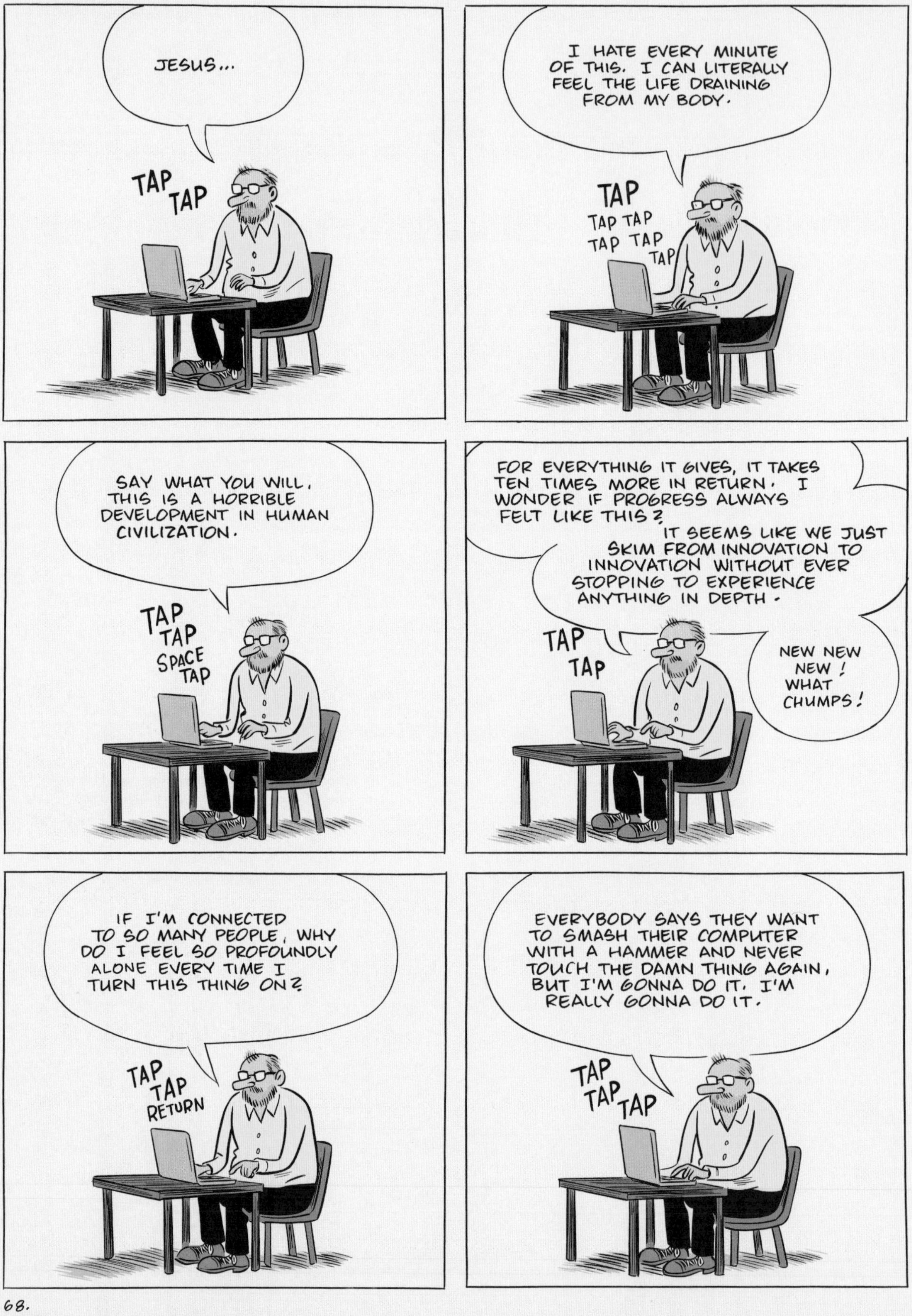
JESUS...
TAP TAP
I HATE EVERY MINUTE OF THIS. I CAN LITERALLY FEEL THE LIFE DRAINING FROM MY BODY.
TAP TAP TAP TAP TAP TAP
SAY WHAT YOU WILL, THIS IS A HORRIBLE DEVELOPMENT IN HUMAN CIVILIZATION.
TAP TAP SPACE TAP
FOR EVERYTHING IT GIVES, IT TAKES TEN TIMES MORE IN RETURN. I WONDER IF PROGRESS ALWAYS FELT LIKE THIS?
IT SEEMS LIKE WE JUST SKIM FROM INNOVATION TO INNOVATION WITHOUT EVER STOPPING TO EXPERIENCE ANYTHING IN DEPTH.
NEW NEW NEW! WHAT CHUMPS!
TAP TAP
IF I'M CONNECTED TO SO MANY PEOPLE, WHY DO I FEEL SO PROFOUNDLY ALONE EVERY TIME I TURN THIS THING ON?
TAP TAP RETURN
EVERYBODY SAYS THEY WANT TO SMASH THEIR COMPUTER WITH A HAMMER AND NEVER TOUCH THE DAMN THING AGAIN, BUT I'M GONNA DO IT. I'M REALLY GONNA DO IT.
TAP TAP TAP

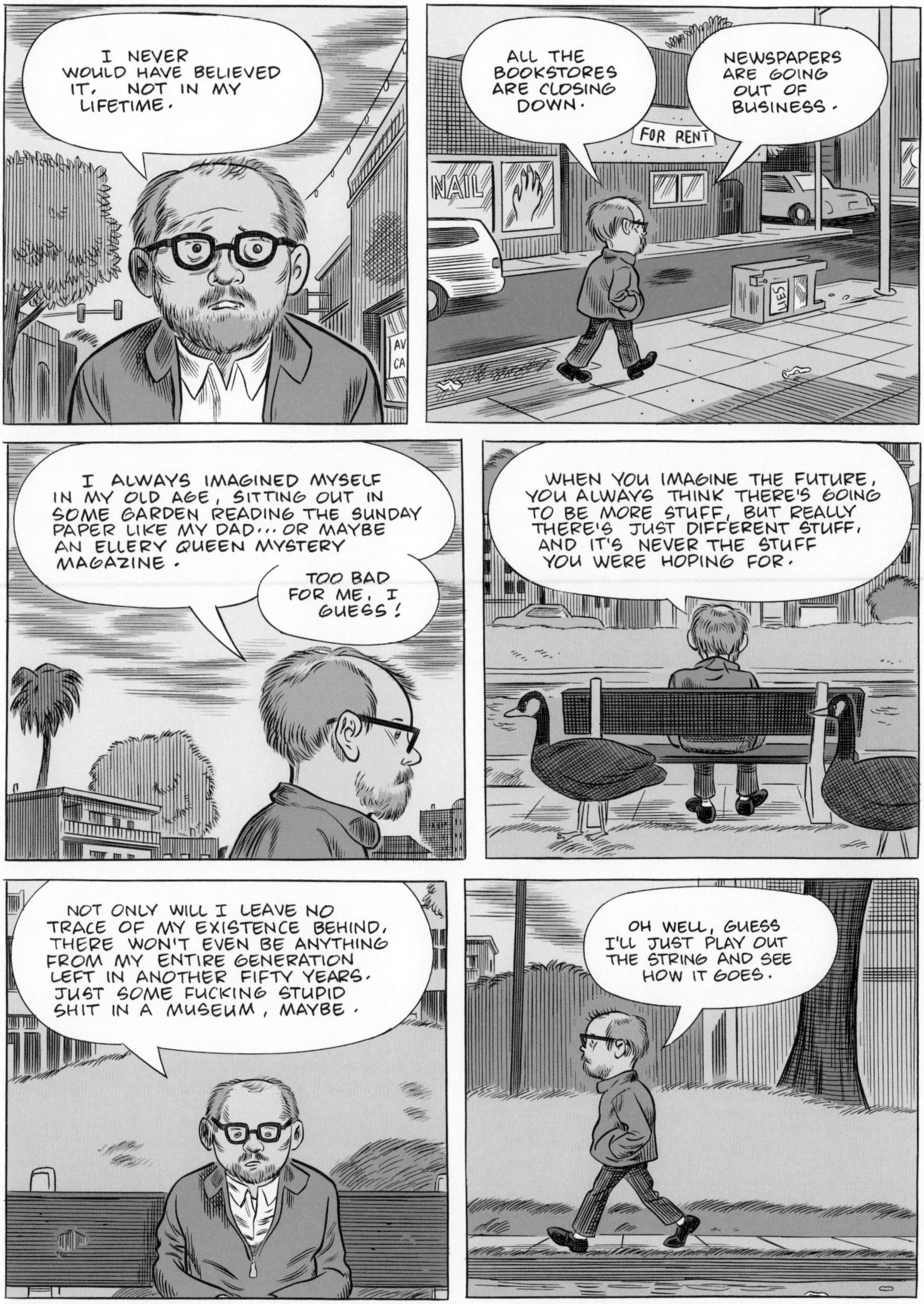
I NEVER WOULD HAVE BELIEVED IT. NOT IN MY LIFETIME.
ALL THE BOOKSTORES ARE CLOSING DOWN.
NEWSPAPERS ARE GOING OUT OF BUSINESS.
FOR RENT
NAIL
I ALWAYS IMAGINED MYSELF IN MY OLD AGE, SITTING OUT IN SOME GARDEN READING THE SUNDAY PAPER LIKE MY DAD... OR MAYBE AN ELLERY QUEEN MYSTERY MAGAZINE.
TOO BAD FOR ME, I GUESS!
WHEN YOU IMAGINE THE FUTURE, YOU ALWAYS THINK THERE'S GOING TO BE MORE STUFF, BUT REALLY THERE'S JUST DIFFERENT STUFF, AND IT'S NEVER THE STUFF YOU WERE HOPING FOR.
NOT ONLY WILL I LEAVE NO TRACE OF MY EXISTENCE BEHIND, THERE WON'T EVEN BE ANYTHING FROM MY ENTIRE GENERATION LEFT IN ANOTHER FIFTY YEARS. JUST SOME FUCKING STUPID SHIT IN A MUSEUM, MAYBE.
OH WELL, GUESS I'LL JUST PLAY OUT THE STRING AND SEE HOW IT GOES.

CALLER I.D.

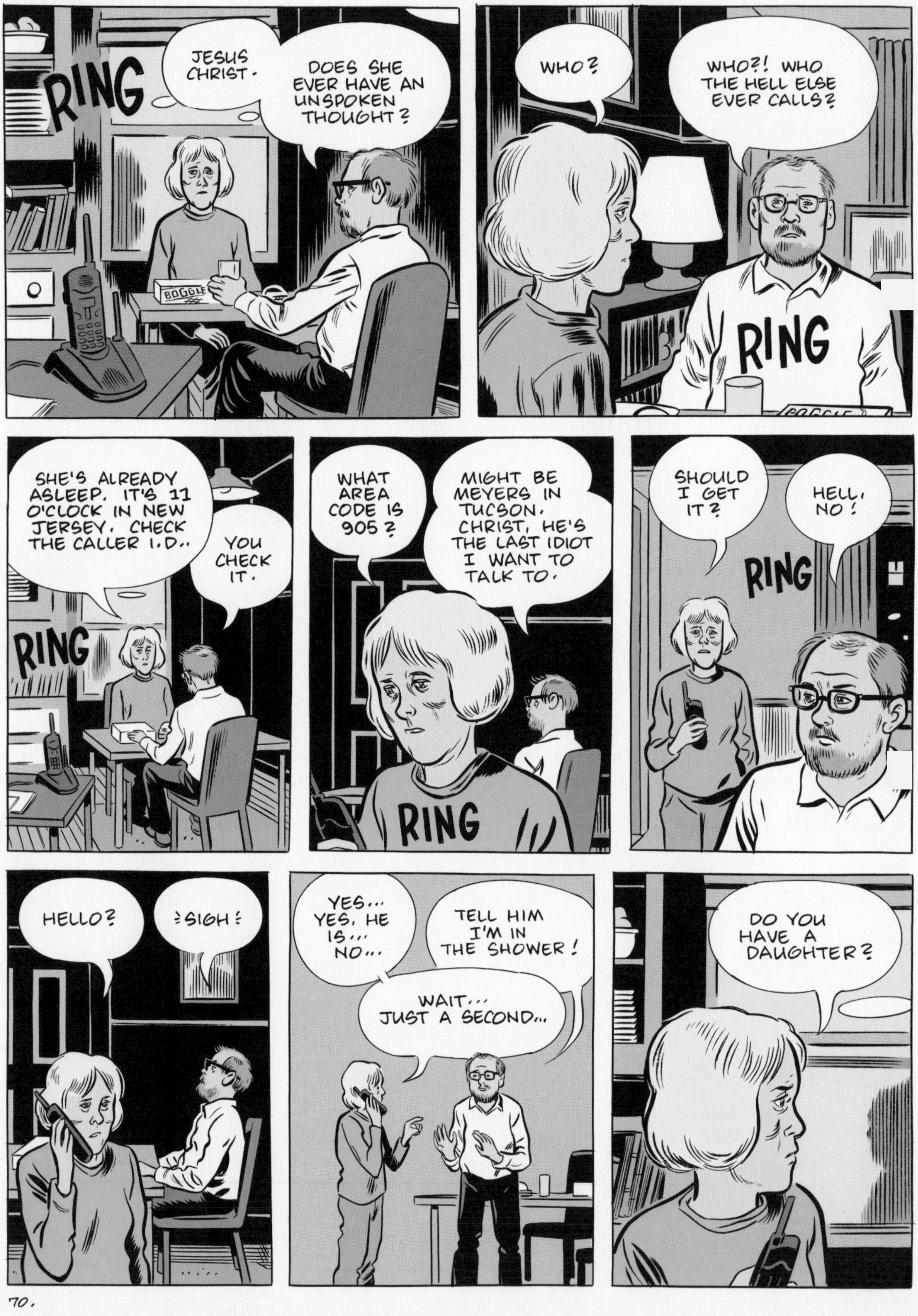
RING
JESUS CHRIST.
DOES SHE EVER HAVE AN UNSPOKEN THOUGHT?
BOGGLE
WHO?
WHO?! WHO THE HELL ELSE EVER CALLS?
RING
SHE'S ALREADY ASLEEP. IT'S 11 O'CLOCK IN NEW JERSEY. CHECK THE CALLER I.D..
YOU CHECK IT.
RING
WHAT AREA CODE IS 905?
MIGHT BE MEYERS IN TUCSON. CHRIST, HE'S THE LAST IDIOT I WANT TO TALK TO.
RING
SHOULD I GET IT?
HELL, NO!
RING
HELLO?
SIGH
YES... YES, HE IS... NO...
TELL HIM I'M IN THE SHOWER!
WAIT... JUST A SECOND...
DO YOU HAVE A DAUGHTER?

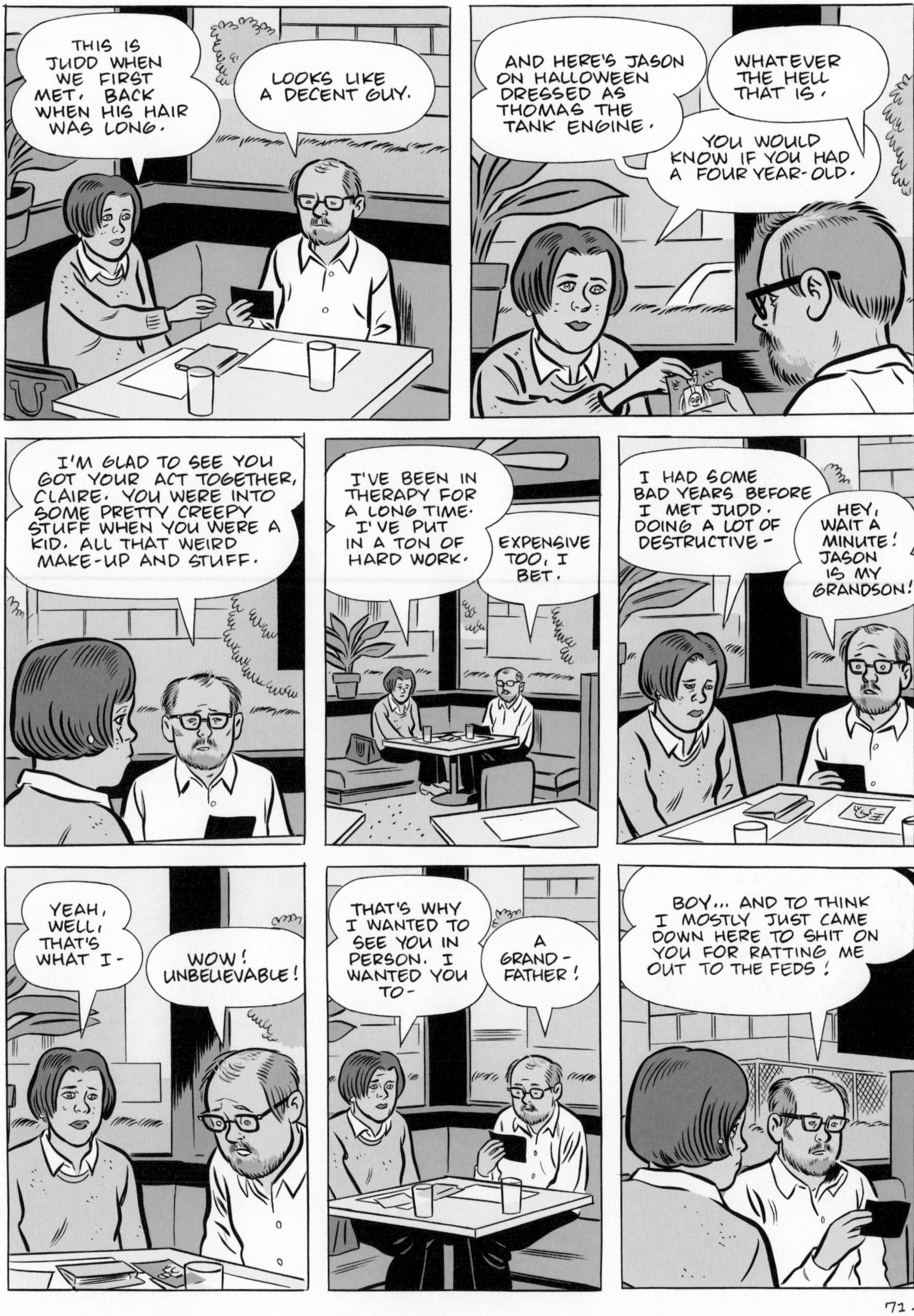
THIS IS JUDD WHEN WE FIRST MET, BACK WHEN HIS HAIR WAS LONG.
LOOKS LIKE A DECENT GUY.
AND HERE'S JASON ON HALLOWEEN DRESSED AS THOMAS THE TANK ENGINE.
WHATEVER THE HELL THAT IS.
YOU WOULD KNOW IF YOU HAD A FOUR YEAR-OLD.
I'M GLAD TO SEE YOU GOT YOUR ACT TOGETHER, CLAIRE. YOU WERE INTO SOME PRETTY CREEPY STUFF WHEN YOU WERE A KID. ALL THAT WEIRD MAKE-UP AND STUFF.
I'VE BEEN IN THERAPY FOR A LONG TIME. I'VE PUT IN A TON OF HARD WORK.
EXPENSIVE TOO, I BET.
I HAD SOME BAD YEARS BEFORE I MET JUDD. DOING A LOT OF DESTRUCTIVE -
HEY, WAIT A MINUTE! JASON IS MY GRANDSON!
YEAH, WELL, THAT'S WHAT I -
WOW! UNBELIEVABLE!
THAT'S WHY I WANTED TO SEE YOU IN PERSON. I WANTED YOU TO-
A GRAND-FATHER!
BOY... AND TO THINK I MOSTLY JUST CAME DOWN HERE TO SHIT ON YOU FOR RATTING ME OUT TO THE FEDS!

HAIRCUT

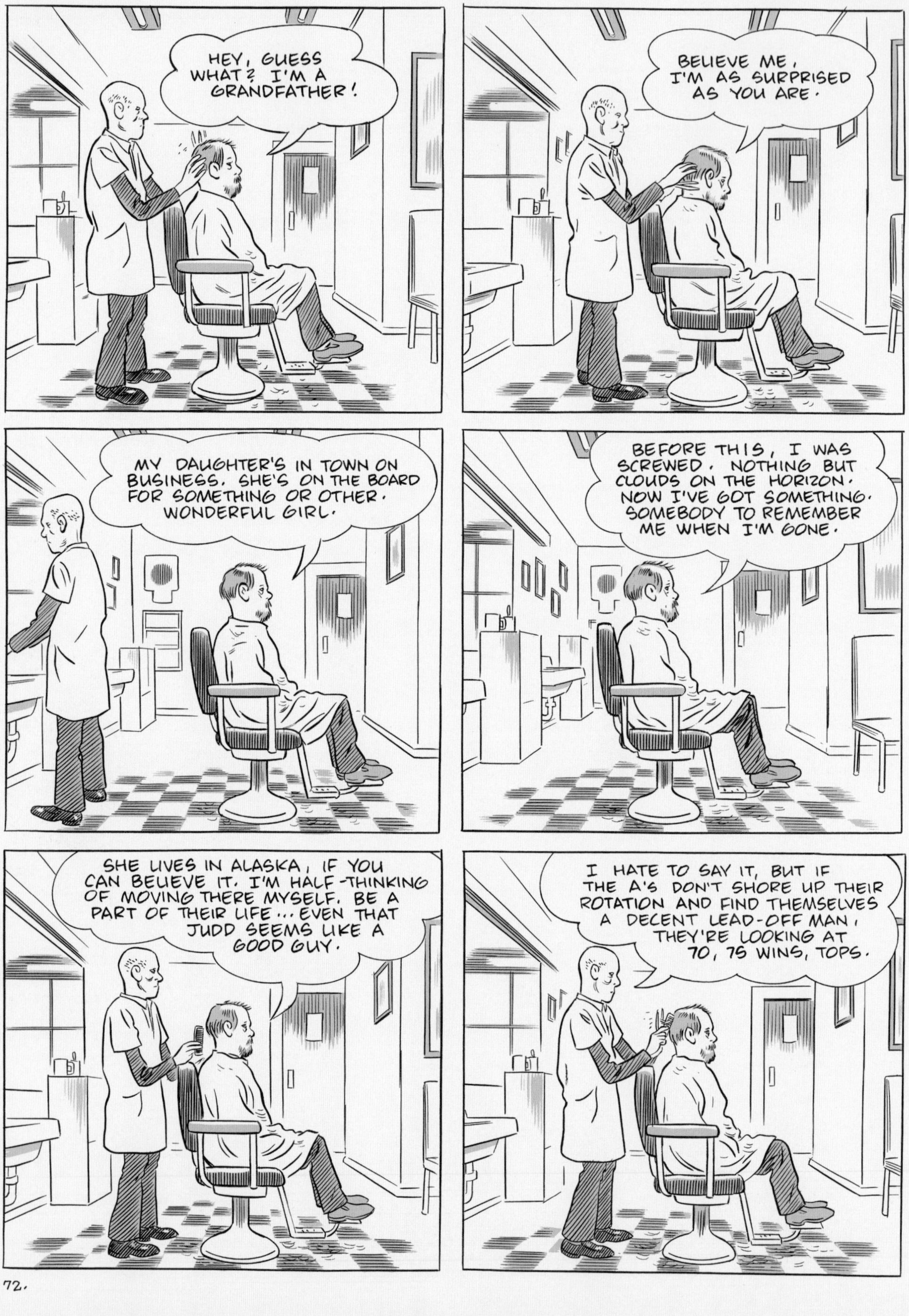
HEY, GUESS WHAT? I'M A GRANDFATHER!
BELIEVE ME, I'M AS SURPRISED AS YOU ARE.
MY DAUGHTER'S IN TOWN ON BUSINESS. SHE'S ON THE BOARD FOR SOMETHING OR OTHER. WONDERFUL GIRL.
BEFORE THIS, I WAS SCREWED. NOTHING BUT CLOUDS ON THE HORIZON. NOW I'VE GOT SOMETHING. SOMEBODY TO REMEMBER ME WHEN I'M GONE.
SHE LIVES IN ALASKA, IF YOU CAN BELIEVE IT. I'M HALF-THINKING OF MOVING THERE MYSELF. BE A PART OF THEIR LIFE... EVEN THAT JUDD SEEMS LIKE A GOOD GUY.
I HATE TO SAY IT, BUT IF THE A'S DON'T SHORE UP THEIR ROTATION AND FIND THEMSELVES A DECENT LEAD-OFF MAN, THEY'RE LOOKING AT 70, 75 WINS, TOPS.

THE TRAIL

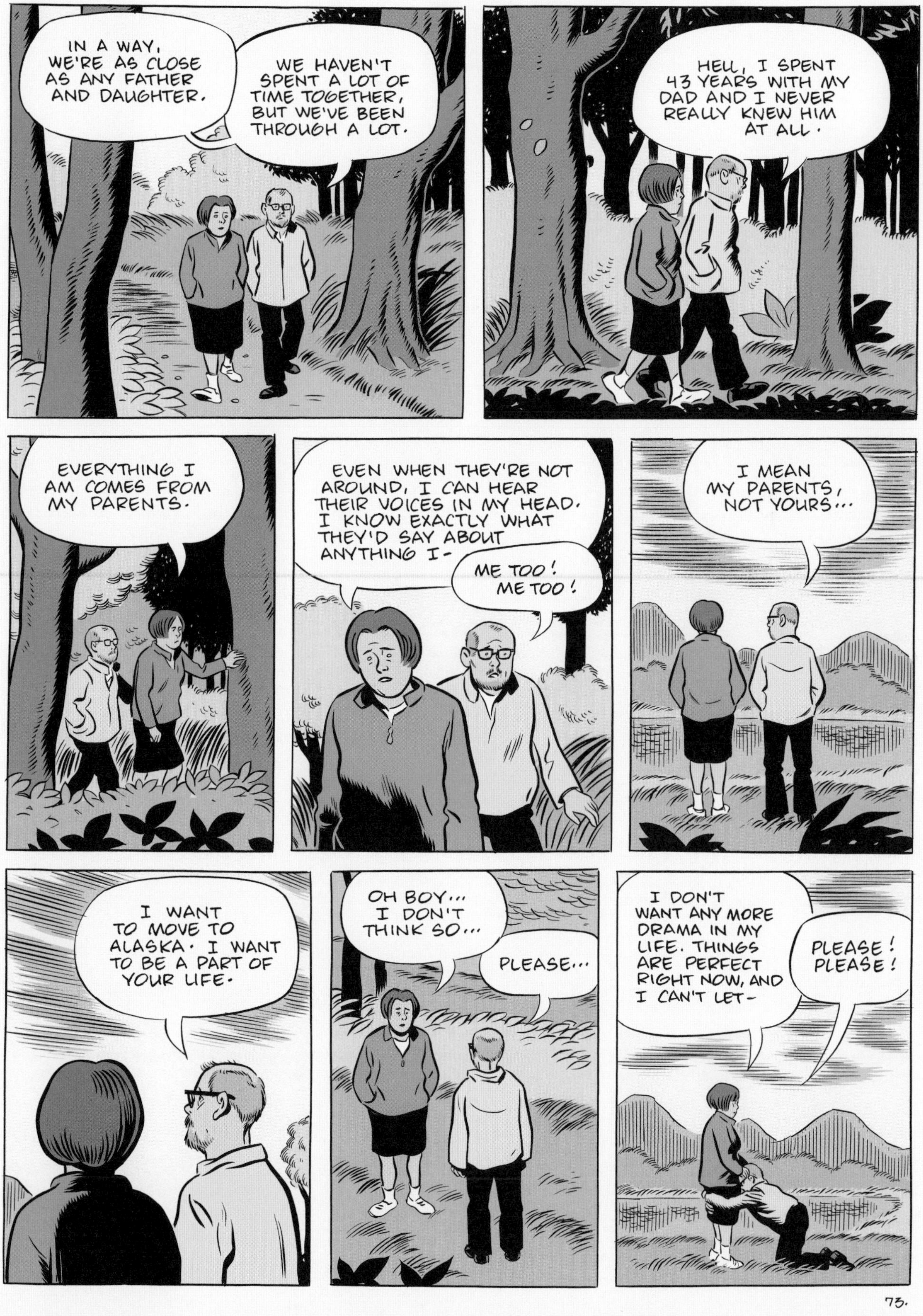
IN A WAY, WE'RE AS CLOSE AS ANY FATHER AND DAUGHTER.
WE HAVEN'T SPENT A LOT OF TIME TOGETHER, BUT WE'VE BEEN THROUGH A LOT.
HELL, I SPENT 43 YEARS WITH MY DAD AND I NEVER REALLY KNEW HIM AT ALL.
EVERYTHING I AM COMES FROM MY PARENTS.
EVEN WHEN THEY'RE NOT AROUND, I CAN HEAR THEIR VOICES IN MY HEAD. I KNOW EXACTLY WHAT THEY'D SAY ABOUT ANYTHING I-
ME TOO! ME TOO!
I MEAN MY PARENTS, NOT YOURS...
I WANT TO MOVE TO ALASKA. I WANT TO BE A PART OF YOUR LIFE.
OH BOY... I DON'T THINK SO...
PLEASE...
I DON'T WANT ANY MORE DRAMA IN MY LIFE. THINGS ARE PERFECT RIGHT NOW, AND I CAN'T LET-
PLEASE! PLEASE!

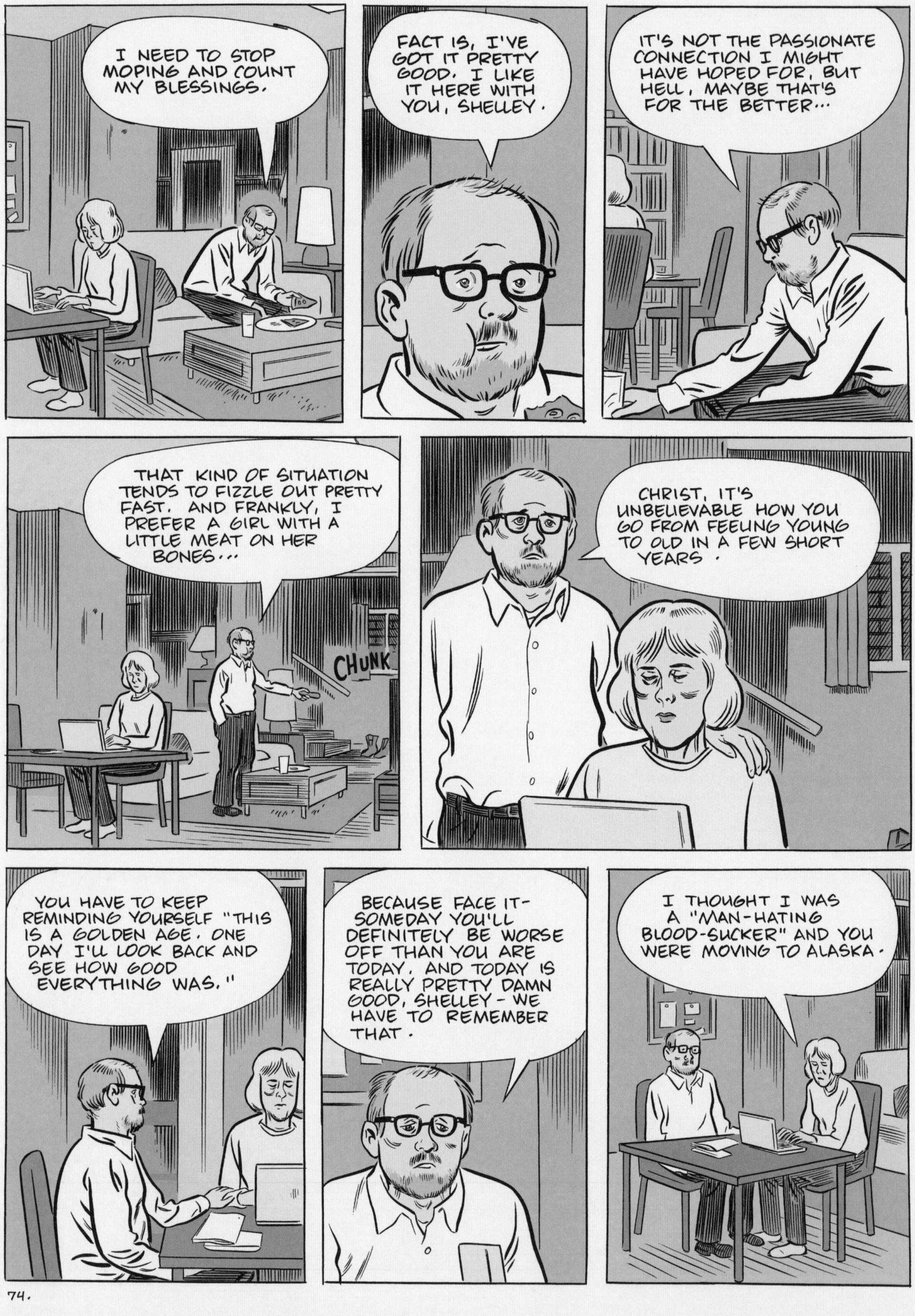
I NEED TO STOP MOPING AND COUNT MY BLESSINGS.
FACT IS, I'VE GOT IT PRETTY GOOD. I LIKE IT HERE WITH YOU, SHELLEY.
IT'S NOT THE PASSIONATE CONNECTION I MIGHT HAVE HOPED FOR, BUT HELL, MAYBE THAT'S FOR THE BETTER...
THAT KIND OF SITUATION TENDS TO FIZZLE OUT PRETTY FAST. AND FRANKLY, I PREFER A GIRL WITH A LITTLE MEAT ON HER BONES...
CHUNK
CHRIST, IT'S UNBELIEVABLE HOW YOU GO FROM FEELING YOUNG TO OLD IN A FEW SHORT YEARS.
YOU HAVE TO KEEP REMINDING YOURSELF "THIS IS A GOLDEN AGE. ONE DAY I'LL LOOK BACK AND SEE HOW GOOD EVERYTHING WAS."
BECAUSE FACE IT- SOMEDAY YOU'LL DEFINITELY BE WORSE OFF THAN YOU ARE TODAY, AND TODAY IS REALLY PRETTY DAMN GOOD, SHELLEY - WE HAVE TO REMEMBER THAT.
I THOUGHT I WAS A "MAN-HATING BLOOD-SUCKER" AND YOU WERE MOVING TO ALASKA.

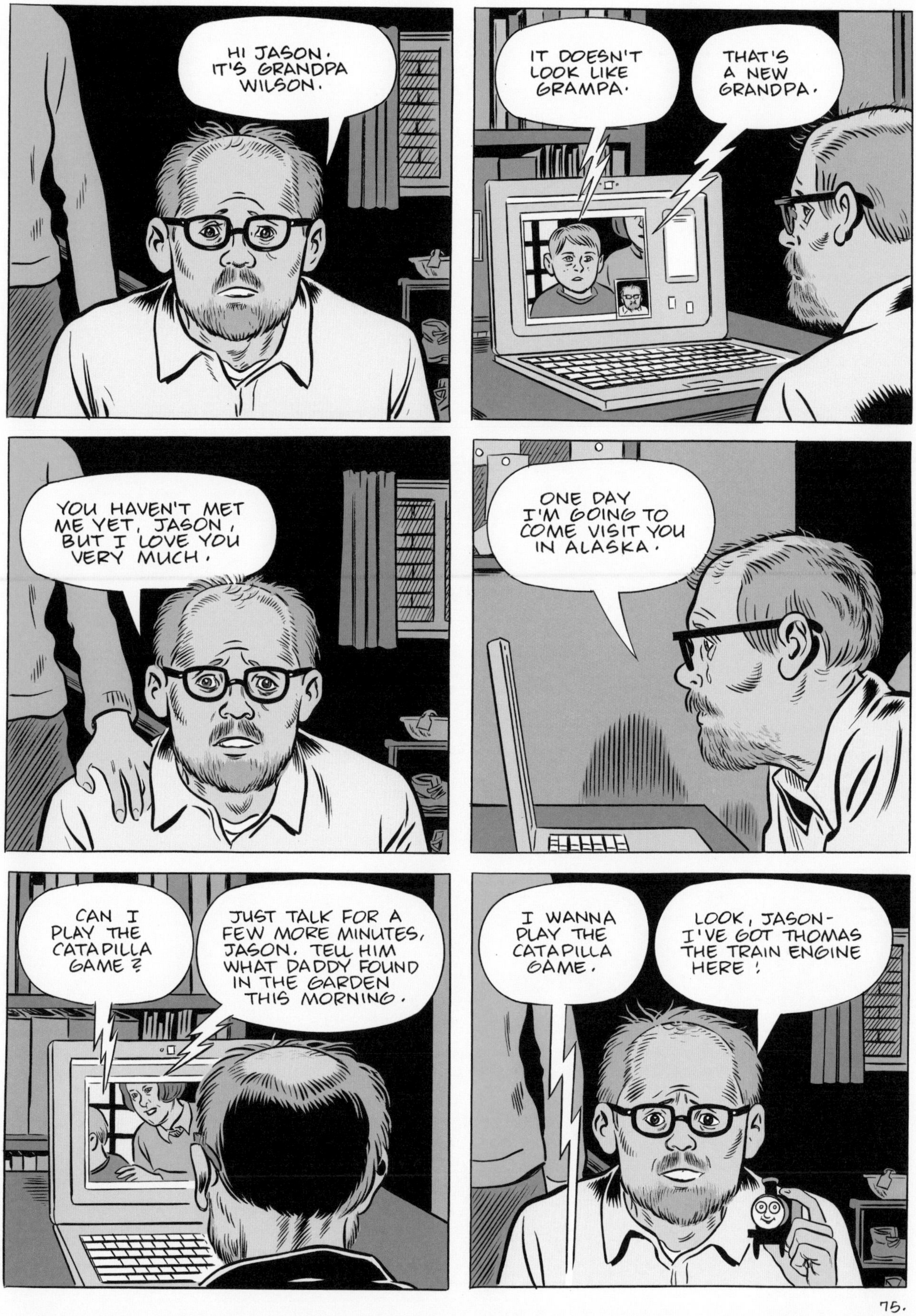
HI JASON. IT'S GRANDPA WILSON.
IT DOESN'T LOOK LIKE GRAMPA.
THAT'S A NEW GRANDPA.
YOU HAVEN'T MET ME YET, JASON, BUT I LOVE YOU VERY MUCH.
ONE DAY I'M GOING TO COME VISIT YOU IN ALASKA.
CAN I PLAY THE CATAPILLA GAME?
JUST TALK FOR A FEW MORE MINUTES, JASON. TELL HIM WHAT DADDY FOUND IN THE GARDEN THIS MORNING.
I WANNA PLAY THE CATAPILLA GAME.
LOOK, JASON- I'VE GOT THOMAS THE TRAIN ENGINE HERE!

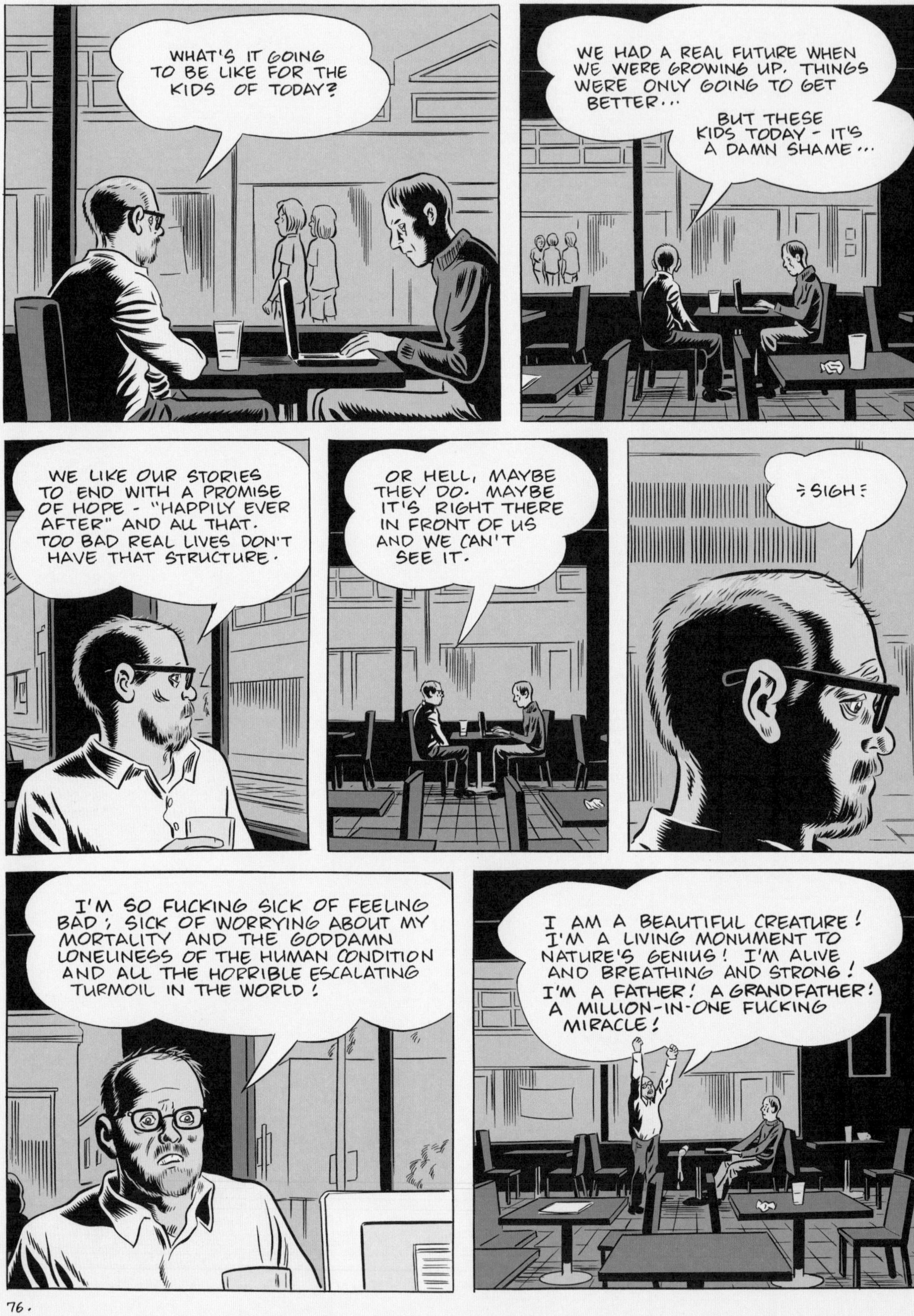
WHAT'S IT GOING TO BE LIKE FOR THE KIDS OF TODAY?
WE HAD A REAL FUTURE WHEN WE WERE GROWING UP. THINGS WERE ONLY GOING TO GET BETTER...
BUT THESE KIDS TODAY - IT'S A DAMN SHAME...
WE LIKE OUR STORIES TO END WITH A PROMISE OF HOPE - "HAPPILY EVER AFTER" AND ALL THAT. TOO BAD REAL LIVES DON'T HAVE THAT STRUCTURE.
OR HELL, MAYBE THEY DO. MAYBE IT'S RIGHT THERE IN FRONT OF US AND WE CAN'T SEE IT.
SIGH
I'M SO FUCKING SICK OF FEELING BAD; SICK OF WORRYING ABOUT MY MORTALITY AND THE GODDAMN LONELINESS OF THE HUMAN CONDITION AND ALL THE HORRIBLE ESCALATING TURMOIL IN THE WORLD!
I AM A BEAUTIFUL CREATURE! I'M A LIVING MONUMENT TO NATURE'S GENIUS! I'M ALIVE AND BREATHING AND STRONG! I'M A FATHER! A GRANDFATHER! A MILLION-IN-ONE FUCKING MIRACLE!

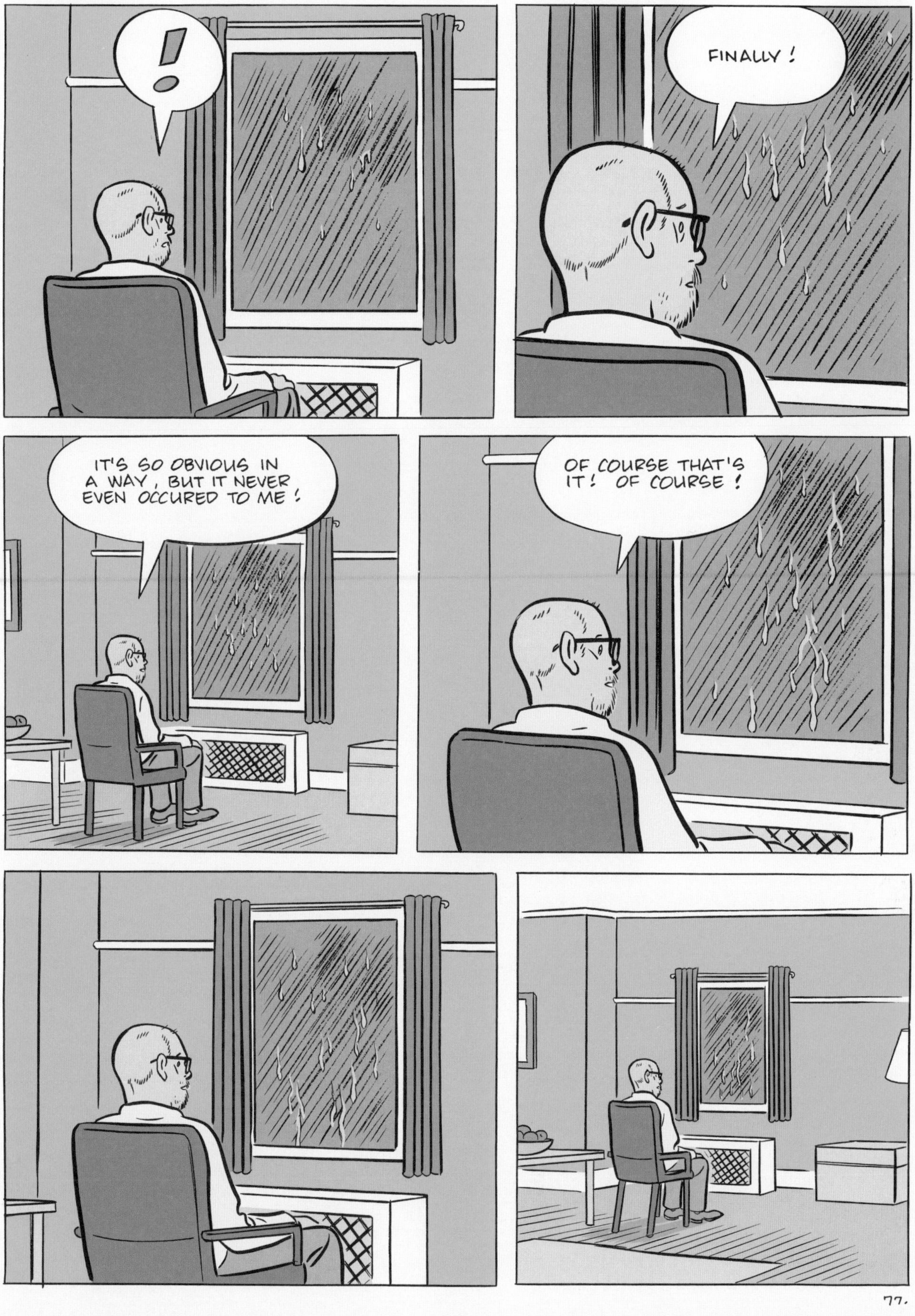
!
FINALLY !
IT'S SO OBVIOUS IN A WAY , BUT IT NEVER EVEN OCCURED TO ME !
OF COURSE THAT'S IT! OF COURSE !

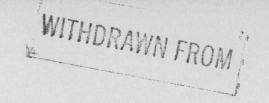

DANIEL CLOWES WAS BORN IN CHICAGO IN 1961. HE IS THE AUTHOR OF SEVERAL BOOKS, INCLUDING GHOST WORLD, ICE HAVEN, DAVID BORING, THE DEATH-RAY, AND PATIENCE. SEVERAL OF THESE WORKS ORIGINALLY APPEARED IN SERIAL FORM IN HIS COMIC-BOOK SERIES, EIGHTBALL, WHICH RAN FOR 23 ISSUES FROM 1989-2004. WILSON WAS HIS FIRST ORIGINAL GRAPHIC NOVEL. HE FINDS IT UNCOMFORTABLE TO HAND-LETTER INFORMATION ABOUT HIMSELF IN THE THIRD PERSON BUT FEELS THE NEED TO FILL THIS SPACE WITH A BLOCK OF TEXT FOR DESIGN PURPOSES. HE HAS WRITTEN SEVERAL SCREENPLAYS, INCLUDING THE FILM ADAPTATION OF THIS VERY BOOK. MORE INFORMATION ABOUT THIS FASCINATING FELLOW CAN BE FOUND AT WWW.DANIELCLOWES.COM. HE LIVES IN OAKLAND, CA, WITH HIS WIFE, ERIKA, AND SON, CHARLIE.